AVRO LANCASTER

Text by BILL SWEETMAN / Illustrations by RIKYU WATANABE

Jane's Publishing Company Limited
London · Sydney

Fraser-Nash FN.50 mid upper turret

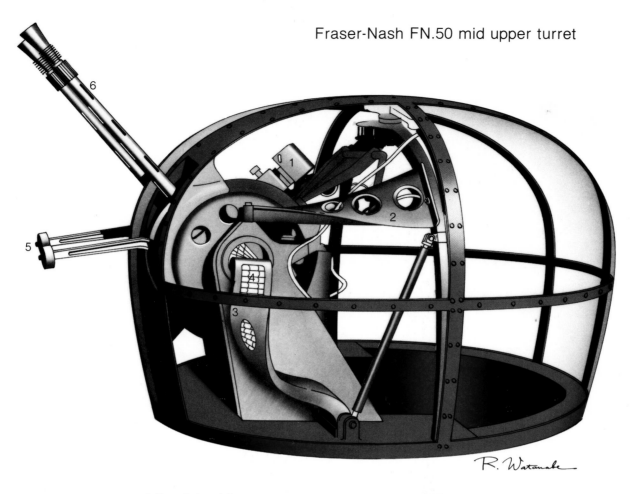

R. Watanabe

1 Gun aiming sight
2 Left side support arm
3 Left side ammunition duct
4 Ammunition belt
5 Gun barrel stoppers
6 Two Browning 0.303 in (7.7 mm) machine-guns

This book was designed and produced by Wing & Anchor Press,
a division of Zokeisha Publications, Ltd.
5-1-6, Roppongi, Minato-ku, Tokyo 106/123 East 54th Street, New York 10022.

© 1982 by Zokeisha Publications, Ltd.

First published in Great Britain by Jane's Publishing Company, Ltd.,
238 City Road, London, EC1V 2PU.

Printed and bound in Japan.
First printing, April, 1982.

ISBN No. 0 7106 0132 8

Lancaster I, SR-Z, of No.101 Squadron about to take off. The aircraft is equipped with the H2S radar bombing system.

(Imperial War Museum)

Introduction

The Avro Lancaster bomber is one of the most significant combat aircraft to have taken part in World War II. The legend of British technological invincibility that has grown up around the raid by 617 Squadron on the Ruhr dams in 1943, and the resulting popular fame of the Lancaster, have tended to obscure its true importance.

That the Lancaster was an outstanding design among its contemporaries was realised during 1941, when the design emerged from the heavy, ugly chrysalis of the Manchester. That a direct descendant of the design would still be in first-line service with the RAF in 1982, nearly half a century after the original specification was issued, was then unimaginable.

The Lancaster was never intended as a multi-role aircraft. Together with its descendant, the Lancaster IV/V or Lincoln, it formed the basis of a number of transport aircraft which ranged from the mediocre to the dangerously useless. Notwithstanding the sterling qualities of the Shackleton it was hardly considered in the same class as the contemporary Neptune.

There was, however, one quality in which the Lancaster was genuinely outstanding – its supreme suitability for its intended role. The leaders of Bomber Command wanted to deliver large quantities of explosives and incendiaries to German cities, at night and without an escort. By virtue of its slow speed such an aircraft was vulnerable to damage or destruction by the defences. The Lancaster was tough and able to survive attacks, simple in construction for easy repair if it came home damaged, and easy to build in quantity, to replace the aircraft which never returned. It was the ideal bomb truck, with a far greater weapons load than any of its contemporaries. For an aircraft designed in 1936, its ability to carry its payload and more in the form of a single weapon was extraordinary. The bomber's handling, although not faultless, was to prove reasonably unaffected by the high operating weights.

It could be argued that the history of Bomber Command would have been very different had it not been for the Lancaster. Had the Manchester not been developed into the Lancaster with such unexpected success, Bomber Command would have had nothing better than the Halifax, and the crisis of early 1944 would have come a great deal earlier, possibly proving too great a defeat for the advocates of area bombing for the policy to survive.

The evolution of the Lancaster presents an interesting contrast to the development in Germany of the contemporary Heinkel He177 heavy bomber. The He177 was developed to a specification issued in 1936, like the Manchester, and flown in the same year as the British bomber. It was a twin-engined heavy bomber similarly plagued by troubles with heavy, complicated engines, which had an unfortunate tendency to catch fire. Design teams at Rostock and Manchester were roughing out the lines of modified aircraft with four smaller, more reliable powerplants in early 1940, but whereas the Manchester III prototype made its first flight in January 1941 and was selected for production within a matter of months, the parallel He177 did not appear until the end of 1943. By that time it was too late.

The Lancaster's greatest significance, however, was that it was both the last of the old generation and the first of the new. Designed for an Air Staff which believed that the bomber was invincible and still envisaged the bomber as a slow and heavily armed aerial battleship, the Lancaster first demonstrated that the bomber was vulnerable, and that the hopes of the bomber enthusiasts had been wildly exaggerated. Later, it was to show the way to what the bomber was eventually to become – a stealthy intruder rather than a brazen raider, concealing itself behind subtle electronic smokescreens and finding its way along webs of electromagnetic waves.

By 1945, the British Air Staff had turned from the blinkered and self-deluded supporters of the pre-war heavy bombers to embrace some of the most advanced thinking in the world on the best way to penetrate an enemy's airspace. Never again did a new British bomber carry a single defensive gun – speed, altitude, stealth and, above all, electronic countermeasures were to assure the bomber's ability to penetrate defences. Many of the devices used to the present day on Chadwick's last design, the extraordinary Vulcan, are descendants of the mysterious black boxes developed for Bomber Command Lancasters. The Avro bomber contributed greatly to the history of aviation in testing out the tremendous changes in bomber philosophy, by its continued and dogged service over Germany.

The ultimate weapon

On the 14th anniversary of the armistice which ended the Great War of 1914–18, a leading article in *The Times* of London dealt with the subject of aerial warfare. "The supreme menace and the supreme horror of war comes from the air," intoned the Thunderer, "and unless Mars can. be dethroned in the sky, there will be small gain in pinpricking him on the earth and sea." *The Times*, in short, was calling for international agreement to abolish or severely restrict the use of the bomber aircraft, in terms which are more familiar in the modern world from the opponents of nuclear weapons.

The fear of the bomber which was prevalent in the 1930s was something very different from the apprehension aroused by more conventional, familiar problems of defence such as land war in Europe or the defence of sea lanes. One reason for the extent of this fear was that in the past there was very little evidence of the effects of air attacks on any large scale, the forays of Imperial Germany's airships and bombers having been little more than experimental operations. Since that time bomber fleets had expanded, and there were clear signs that the aeroplane was on the point of evolution into a far more reliable, faster machine, carrying a much greater load. Above all, however, the bomber's range and mobility gave an enemy the chance to carry the war to the homes of the civilian population in a way which only slow land war or invasion could have done before.

It was this last aspect of bomber warfare which particularly alarmed the British. Despite their pride in a 900-year clean record in defeating would-be invaders, and their professed faith in the invincibility of the Royal Navy, the British had become used to terrifying their children with the threat of the foreign invader ("Bonaparte may come this way", concluded a 19th-century nursery rhyme) and could also panic themselves, as in 1870 and the early 1900s. The idea of a bomber force sailing impudently over the iron walls of the Home Fleet was enough to tie the stomach of the body politic in a sickening knot.

Bomber phobia was not confined to the general public or even to the politicians. One internal memorandum within the Admiralty went so far as to describe the bombing of civilian populations as "revolting and un-English". The effectiveness of air attack was a controversial subject among military experts, and there were many who supported and encouraged popular fears. Generally, however, the British Admiralty and the War Office (which controlled the Army) were reluctant to concede that bombing would be effective at all. This attitude was based less on detailed studies of bombing techniques than on resentment of the funds being appropriated by the Air Ministry for the development of the Royal Air Force's Heyford and Hendon bombers.

Urged by the public and the Foreign Office, the government of Stanley Baldwin took the view that the effect of bombing could be devastating, even to the point where a heavy air attack could cause civilian morale to collapse and force surrender before land or sea battle could be joined. The question was what to do about it. The politicians' view was that bombing should be curtailed by international agreement, and preliminary discussions under the auspices of the League of Nations were held in Geneva in February 1932. Baldwin himself took the extreme view that all bombing should be abolished, and civil aviation discouraged by the removal of subsidies in order to slow the advance of aeronautical technology. More moderate proposals included the international control of commercial aviation, and a ban on bomber research and development. This was seen as entirely practicable; warships, after all, were already limited by international agreement.

In the worsening international tensions of the early 1930s, and in particular with the realisation that Germany's National Socialist government – elected in 1933 – would not be a party to any agreement on restricting bombers, the opposing view of the Air Ministry began to gather weight. The Air Ministry had opposed any ban on bombing from the start, because it argued that the bomber was the cheapest and most efficient way of policing the North-West Frontier. Moreover, it preached that devastating air attack was inevitable in the event of war. The only defence, the Air Ministry said, was counter-attack, and this was reflected in the RAF expansion which started in 1934.

The first steps in RAF expansion were rightly identified by Lord Swinton, Secretary of State for Air in the early years of the expansion programme, as the enlargement of the industrial base and the RAF's human and fixed resources rather than the development of new aircraft types. The first of the expansion schemes were based on the obsolete Hendon and Heyford. Scheme C of 1935 included the Whitley and Harrow, both developed from existing "bomber-transport" prototypes, while the newer Wellington and Hampden would follow in later schemes.

These two later aircraft were already well into their development by late 1935, when the eyes of the British Air Staff turned enviously westwards. July 1935 had seen the first flight of the Boeing 299 bomber. The first four-engined aircraft to use modern aerodynamic and constructional technology, the 299 – later to become the B-17 – displayed a combination of defensive and offensive armament, speed, altitude and range which astonished the aviation world. The Air Staff, under Sir Edward Ellington, asked the Air Ministry to approve development of a new class of heavy bombers superior to the Boeing 299, and the Air Ministry gave its approval in February 1936.

Boeing YB-17, the first production version of the Model 299, in flight.   (USAF)

Because Germany was now regarded as the most likely enemy, a range of at least 2,000 miles (3,200 km) was basic to the new requirements. The new bombers were also expected to be able to defend themselves in daylight, as were the Wellington and Hampden. However, they were able to take advantage of a weapon in which Britain had established an early and valuable lead, and in which Bomber Command placed great faith – the powered gun turret.

The powered turret had been developed by two ex-Royal Flying Corps pilots, "Tommy" Thompson and "Archie" Frazer-Nash. The latter was an engineer of no mean ability, and the designer of the unconventional but much admired chain transmission of the sports cars which bore his name. Foreseeing that the only way in which defensive guns could be used on high-speed aircraft was to power the guns in elevation and traverse against the force of the slipstream, Frazer-Nash and Thompson obtained a contract to fit an experimental turret to a Hawker Demon fighter in 1933. This early start was important, because the development of the powered turret was not easy – the movement of the guns had to be smooth and manageable at low speeds for aiming and tracking, but had to move fast for acquiring a new threat from another quarter. The size and weight restriction compounded the engineering and production problems, but from the formation of the Nash & Thompson company to build turrets in early 1935, production built up steadily and was in full swing by 1939.

The new RAF bombers combined the speed of the day bombers with a greater weapon load than the slower night bombers – such as the Whitley and Harrow – and a heavy defensive armament. In July 1936 the Air Staff issued two specifications for the new "heavies" and invited manufacturers to compete for contracts. One of the specifications, B.12/36, was relatively conservative, calling for some increase in performance over the Boeing 299, using four engines derived from types then well advanced in development. In the summer of 1937 prototypes to B.12/36 were ordered from Shorts and from Vickers-Supermarine. The former was to become the Stirling, but the Supermarine 318 lost development priority to the Spitfire and was abandoned in 1940 after a bombing raid destroyed the partly completed prototype.

The other specification was P.13/36, and as the prefix implied it called for prototypes rather than a production bomber, being rather more advanced and more risky than B.12/36. More a "heavy-medium" bomber than a heavy, P.13/36 was designed to be very fast, with a cruising speed of 275 mph (443 km/hr), and a range of 3,000 miles (4,830 km) with a 4,000 lb (1,800 kg) load. Powered turrets were to be installed in the nose and tail. High speed was to be attained by high wing loading, and by the use of new engines in the 2,000 hp class – twice the power of the Merlin, which was then starting flight tests in the Hurricane and Spitfire. The heavily loaded bomber was to be launched with the aid of a catapult, like a carrier-based aircraft, increasing permissible take-off weight and making a smaller wing possible. Handley Page, suppliers of heavy bombers to the British services since 1915, proposed the HP.56, a derivative of an earlier day-bomber design which had been proposed to the same specification as

the Vickers Warwick, and prototypes of this aircraft were ordered to P.13/36 in early 1937. Rather more surprisingly, the second firm chosen to build an aircraft to P.13/36 was that of A. V. Roe and Company, trading as Avro.

Avro was second only to Shorts in seniority among the British aircraft industry. Alliott Verdon-Roe – later knighted for his achievements – became the first Briton to fly an all-British aeroplane in July 1909 and was promptly threatened with prosecution as a danger to public safety. Roe's subsequent efforts were more successful. His Type E biplane of 1912 was the basis for the Avro 504. After a brief combat career, the 504 became the Royal Air Force's standard trainer, until it was replaced in the late 1920s by another Avro machine, the Tutor.

Avro had gained some experience with larger aircraft in the late 1920s, when the company took out a licence to build the Fokker F.VIIB/3m tri-motor transport as the Avro Ten. One of the first monoplane airliners to be built in Britain, the Ten was followed by the smaller Avro Five (designed along Fokker lines by Avro's chief designer Roy Chadwick), and the Avro 642. The company's first substantial success with larger aircraft, however, was the Avro 652. Structurally similar to the early Fokker-based designs, with a one-piece wooden wing, the 652 differed from them in being a low-wing aircraft with a retractable undercarriage. By the time Chadwick was preparing the company's P.13/36 design, the 652 had been adopted by Coastal Command as the Anson maritime-reconnaissance aircraft, entering service in 1936 as the RAF's first type with retractable landing gear. Nevertheless, the Avro P.13/36, known to the company as the Type 679, was more than four times the size of any aircraft the company had designed before, and was moreover the first Avro aircraft to be built in metal. The attention to the industrial base which had been part of the early RAF expansion plans had paid off – as the Avro P.13/36 prototype was assembled, Avro's workforce under the leadership of Roy Dobson (later to head the company), was gaining experience and growing in size through a production contract for Blenheims, and factory buildings near the Newton Heath plant were being taken over by the rapidly growing aircraft company. Employees numbered 5,000 by August 1938, when Secretary of State for Air Sir Kingsley Wood announced that £1 million was to be invested in a new factory for Avro, and that the workforce would be doubled by mid-1939.

Avro's star was rising so dramatically mainly because of some important changes in British aviation policy. RAF expansion Scheme J had been approved in October 1937 by Lord Swinton, then the Secretary of State for Air, and reflected concern about the growing numbers of Luftwaffe bombers. Scheme J proposed the creation of a numerically equal RAF bomber force by mid-1941, before the P.13/36 designs would be ready for production, but it was rejected by the British Cabinet in favour of greater fighter output. Swinton was replaced as Air Minister by Sir Kingsley Wood in May 1938.

Although fighters had temporarily been granted priority over bombers, the long-term importance of offensive air power was not seriously questioned. More bombers would be bought, but because they would be acquired rather later than Swinton had envisaged they could include a greater proportion of new types such as the P.13/36 and B.12/36. While this policy was evolving, a team of Air Staff officers prepared a paper on "The Ideal Bomber" which had a considerable influence on Air Staff planning, particularly in its advocacy of a few, powerful bombers rather than a numerically larger force of smaller aircraft. In the summer of 1938, the Air Ministry prepared Scheme M, covering the expansion of the RAF up to early 1942. It was expected by that time that the bomber squadrons would very nearly reach the strength proposed for mid-1941 in Swinton's rejected scheme. The equipment planned for these squadrons represented an even bolder gamble, because the Air Ministry wanted to order 500 heavy bombers off the drawing board, among them 200 Avro P.13/36 types.

The cost and boldness of this plan led to queries from some Cabinet members. However, the Air Ministry's mind was made up. Swinton's 1937 scheme had aimed at numerical parity with the Luftwaffe's bombers, but now the Air Ministry wanted an equivalent total bombload, and this could be achieved by a smaller force of heavy bombers. Economies would be possible in flying time, maintenance, accessories and, most important, the number of pilots required. Casualties would also be reduced, because the heavies could carry a satisfactory defensive armament. "Developments in recent years," the Air Ministry hinted to Cabinet, had somewhat reduced the threat of air attack to Britain, and the absolute priority to fighters could be relaxed – even the Cabinet was not openly told of the existence of radar. The heavy-bomber contracts were approved, and hence the expansion of Avro went ahead.

British aircraft production was to be led by the experienced aircraft companies, but in addition to their new and existing factories they organised production in facilities owned by the motor and general engineering industries. Production of the Avro P.13/36 was to be carried out by Avro itself, in charge of a group including Metropolitan-Vickers and Rootes. In November 1938, delicate negotiations started to enable British bomber designs to be produced in Canada. Although there were domestic political objections to the overseas funding of military programmes, it was finally agreed that a consortium of Canadian companies would cut their teeth on the Hampden before putting one of the British heavies into production.

The new heavy bombers were developed under a mantle of secrecy unprecedented in peacetime experience, because of the Air Ministry's fear that their existence might spur Germany into developing a rival strategic bomber force. As it happened, German work on heavy bombers remained half-hearted, the Do19 and Ju89 *Ural-Bomber* programmes being terminated in 1937 and the He177, which replaced them in Luftwaffe planning, being fatally compromised in favour of the tactical-support role. The very existence of the heavy bombers was ostensibly a secret, although in a country the size of the United Kingdom a large aircraft in flight test is hard to conceal. C. G. Grey of *The Aeroplane* could not resist remarking, in an account of the Shorts factory published just

before the secret Stirling made its first flight, "Unfortunately, these machines are a deadly State secret to everybody except the few hundreds of thousands of people . . . within, say, a 50-mile radius of the Shorts works." Accordingly, there was no champagne Press reception at Woodford when Avro test pilot Capt. H. A. Brown took the first Avro P.13/36 on its maiden flight. British cities provided the theme for the names of the new heavy bombers – the Shorts Stirling, Handley Page Halifax, and now the Avro Manchester.

The problem child

Development of the Manchester coincided with the crisis of 1940, but nevertheless was accorded high priority. The architects of the pre-war expansion schemes had accepted the risks involved in ordering large quantities of aircraft types which had not been flight tested, and Manchester production was built up as flight trials continued. Any modifications found necessary were either incorporated at a later stage in production or could be fitted retrospectively to aircraft already built. Despite the interruptions of the Battle of Britain in the summer of 1940, the first production Manchesters were delivered in October 1940, just over a year after the first flight of the prototype.

The Manchester never attained the ambitious performance envisaged by P.13/36, which had been superseded by B.19/37 for production aircraft. One reason was that the proposals for catapult launching of the Manchester had been discarded as impracticable. Bomber Command operated from new bases far more hurriedly and crudely equipped than the pre-war stations, and the provision and maintenance of massive mechanical launching gear was rejected at an early stage. The abandonment of the catapult played a part in the decision to enlarge substantially the Manchester's wing after early flight trials. New outer wings were fitted to the existing centre-section, increasing the span from 80 ft 2 in (24.43 m) to 90 ft 1 in (27.46 m), and take-off and climb performance were improved at the expense of maximum cruising speed.

Directional stability was inadequate, and the second prototype and subsequent Manchester I sported a stumpy third tailfin above the rear fuselage. Defensive armament had been increased by the addition of a ventral gun turret, again at the expense of speed and range, while combat experience in 1939 dictated the need for more passive protection measures, such as armour and self-sealing fuel tanks. The Manchester began to put on weight, as did nearly every aircraft developed for military purposes around that time. The complexity of the new aircraft also caused problems, the hydraulics giving trouble (so extensive a system was completely new to the British industry) and the undercarriage proving weak-kneed.

All these troubles were overshadowed utterly and comprehensively by the failure of the Manchester's heart, the Rolls-Royce Vulture engine. This had been designed in 1937 as the Derby firm's main contender for the military engine market beyond the Merlin. It was considered then that new and more powerful engines would oust powerplants in the class of the Merlin by the early 1940s, and nobody expected the basic V-12, 27-litre Merlin to stay in production throughout the war and to yield an eventual 2,000 hp in service. All three of Britain's manufacturers of large aero-engines – Rolls-Royce, Bristol and the tiny Napier company – had engines in the 2,000 hp class under development in 1937–38, but in the prevailing climate of rationalisation it seemed unlikely that all three of them would be put into production. The Vulture was, in that respect, of the greatest importance to Rolls-Royce.

The Vulture was an X-type 24-cylinder engine, basically consisting of two of the company's Kestrel V-12s vertically opposed and connected to a single crankshaft. (Nearly all 24-cylinder wartime engines used two crankshafts, either in H or double-V layouts.) In detail, though, it was considerably more advanced than the Kestrel. Rolls-Royce's managing director, Ernest (later Lord) Hives, noted in late 1937 that "to get the Vulture going is going to be a terrific job, the biggest we have ever had to tackle".

One of the problems with the Vulture, from Rolls-Royce's point of view, was that it was too complex an engine for a new "shadow factory" to take on. If the Vulture was to be built on the scale envisaged in early 1937, Rolls-Royce would have to transfer the whole of the Merlin production line to shadow factories, running the risk that the supply of engines for the Hurricane and Spitfire might be interrupted. It may have been the desire to reduce the planned 1940 production of the Vulture which led to the decision to redesign the Handley Page aircraft as the HP.57 with four Merlins, only months after the original P.13/36 prototype contracts went out. This redesigned aircraft was to be the Halifax.

The Vulture posed a dilemma for Rolls-Royce. The company needed it in one sense, because of the threat that the RAF would switch to Napier Sabre and Bristol Centaurus power if Derby backed out of the 2,000 hp business. On the other hand, in 1938 Rolls-Royce recognised some of the development potential of the Merlin, and was working on a more powerful V-12, the Griffon. Not much smaller than the Vulture in terms of capacity and output, the Griffon had one overwhelming advantage over the big 24-cylinder engine – it could be fitted to any aircraft which used Merlins, thanks to some very clever detail design. Concentration on the Merlin, with the Griffon to follow, made a great deal of sense to Rolls-Royce.

The Manchester and the Vulture were irrevocably linked in 1938–39, because neither the Centaurus nor the Sabre had been ordered early enough, or in sufficient quantities, to match Manchester production. By the time it became apparent that the Vulture was a problem-filled engine, the inertia of the production programme was irresistible. The Vulture was just not powerful enough for the now heavier Manchester, yielding only 1,760 hp in its initial service form. The Manchester lost height rapidly on one engine and had a lower service ceiling than even the Hampden, never regarded as the best of pre-war bombers. The engine itself suffered early problems with coolant circulation, but oil circulation presented a far more serious difficulty, leading to seizure of the big ends and broken connecting rods – at best the engine would stop dead, but frequently it would catch fire. One of Rolls-Royce's test pilots was among the victims of the Vulture whilst the company wrestled with the technical problems of the engine.

The engine problems were unsolved when 207 Squadron was reformed at Waddington to operate the top-secret new bomber, the first of the new heavies to enter service. (The Stirling, which had been planned to enter service earlier, was delayed by the loss of the first prototype and a bombing raid on the production line.) The first two aircraft

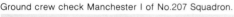 Ground crew check Manchester I of No.207 Squadron.   (Imperial War Museum)

were used for 500 hours of intensive endurance trials in November, and the squadron's next six aircraft were used for Vulture development. It was not until February 24, 1941, a fortnight after the Stirling's operational debut, that the Manchesters of 207 Squadron flew their first operational mission. Six aircraft joined a force of Hampdens to attack enemy shipping at Brest, and one was lost in a landing accident.

The equipment of 207 Squadron comprised basic Manchester Is, but production switched in mid-1941 to the improved Manchester IA. Modified Vultures yielded 1,845 hp at take-off, still with no real reliability, but this barely compensated for the fact that the weight at take-off had risen from 45,000 lb (20,412 kg) for the prototype to 56,000 lb (25,400 kg) on the Manchester IA. Tail armament was increased from two to four machine-guns. The most significant modification, however, was the removal of the central fin and a 50 per cent increase in tailplane span, from 22 ft (6.7 m) to 33 ft (10 m), alleviating the Manchester's stability problems and setting a pattern for future members of the family.

The second Manchester squadron, No 97, became operational in April 1941, three days before a spate of bearing failures in the Vulture caused the grounding of the entire force. Another grounding for modifications to the cooling system followed in June, but the problems continued. Sometimes the airscrews would not feather, turning an engine failure into a slow crash. By that time, although the crews did not know it, the recalcitrant, unreliable, dangerous bomber was dead on its feet. Production and operations nevertheless continued. To the Air Ministry, if not to the crews of 97 and 207 Squadrons, this was preferable to interrupting the re-equipment programme.

Before the P.13/36 flew, Rolls-Royce had concluded internally that a Merlin/Griffon programme would be best for the company. As early as August 1939, Ernest Hives advised the Air Ministry that the Vulture should be scrapped, along with its half-size development, the V-12 Peregrine, and the pressure-air-cooled 24-cylinder Boreas or Exe which the company was developing for the Fairey Firefly naval fighter. The Exe was abandoned, but the other two engines continued in production.

The pressure on the Vulture programme mounted in mid-1940. Lord Beaverbrook, as Minister of Aircraft Production, wanted to rationalise the production of large aero-engines, reducing the number of types in production to five – the two air-cooled Bristol radials (Hercules and Centaurus) and three liquid-cooled units. One of the latter was the Merlin; the Peregrine was certain to be terminated; the Griffon, the Vulture or the Napier Sabre had to go.

While Rolls-Royce wrestled with the Vulture's problems, the full potential of the Napier Sabre was being recognised. Smaller in capacity than the Vulture, and roughly equal in size to the Griffon, the Sabre was promising much higher outputs than either from a tiny, streamlined package of far smaller frontal area than the Rolls-Royce X-24 engine. The Centaurus was also shaping up as a far better engine than the Vulture. Avro had already designed a Manchester II with Bristol or Napier engines, and there seemed little doubt that

the Rolls-Royce Vulture would be ousted from both the Manchester and the new Hawker fighter. The latter, indeed, was eventually produced in quantity with Bristol and Napier engines.

In mid-1940 Hives proposed to the Air Ministry that both his own company's Vulture and the Napier Sabre should be scrapped. Rolls-Royce could continue with the Merlin and the Griffon, while Napier would be deprived of its only product and could slide quietly into history. Whether Rolls-Royce saw the matter in those precise terms is not clear, but the company was clearly worried by the performance of the Sabre, and paid it the ultimate (and for Rolls-Royce, unique) compliment of copying its basic layout for the Griffon's planned successor, the 3,500 hp Eagle. Hives' suggestion was not accepted, and the Vulture and Sabre programmes continued. A few months later, Hives himself rejected a proposal from Rolls-Royce's chairman that an all-out effort to stop the Sabre should be mounted, saying that "the answer to the Sabre is for us to show that the Vulture is a better engine". Whether or not Hives considered that this could be done, in view of the frequent engine failures and airborne conflagrations being experienced by 207 Squadron at that time, is not clear, but at the end of 1940 Rolls-Royce was still committed to production of the Vulture.

The ultimate solution to the problem was beginning to emerge as the Manchester entered service. In September 1940, Rolls-Royce had agreed with Packard to set up a production line for the Merlin in the United States, and the programme went ahead with astonishing speed. Deliveries started within little more than a year of the agreement. Merlin engines would henceforth be in abundant supply.

In the Air Ministry's eyes this removed the main obstacle to production of the Avro Type 683 Manchester III, which had been designed in parallel with the Sabre/Centaurus Manchester II. A Manchester I had been removed from the production line in 1940 for conversion to the Manchester III prototype, and this aircraft was flown on January 9, 1941. The outer wings were extended once more, Merlin X engines in standard Wellington/Whitley/Halifax installations replaced the Vultures, and two extra Merlins were mounted outboard, on simple cantilever frameworks attached to the lower booms of the front and rear spars. Apart from the new outer wings, the Manchester III was structurally identical to the Manchester I.

The success of flight tests with the Manchester III, the apparent inability of Rolls-Royce to solve the Vulture's problems, the availability of abundant Packard Merlins before Sabre or Centaurus engines could be available for a Manchester II, and the urgent need to phase out the Manchester I and IA as soon as possible all pointed in the early months of 1941 to one course of action. By the time the existence of the Manchester was revealed to the British public, in the same month that Metropolitan-Vickers delivered its first production aircraft, and before the second squadron had been declared operational, the decision had been made to end Manchester I development after 200 production aircraft. The remaining 300 aircraft on current contracts would be completed as Manchester IIIs.

Avro Lancaster B.Mk.III

Avro Lancaster B.Mk.III flown by Flight Lieutenant Basil Turner from Skellingthorpe, England in the summer of 1944. The 120 bombing operation marks and the two victories over German aircraft are painted under the cockpit. This plane retired from bombing duties after completing 130 missions in October 1944.

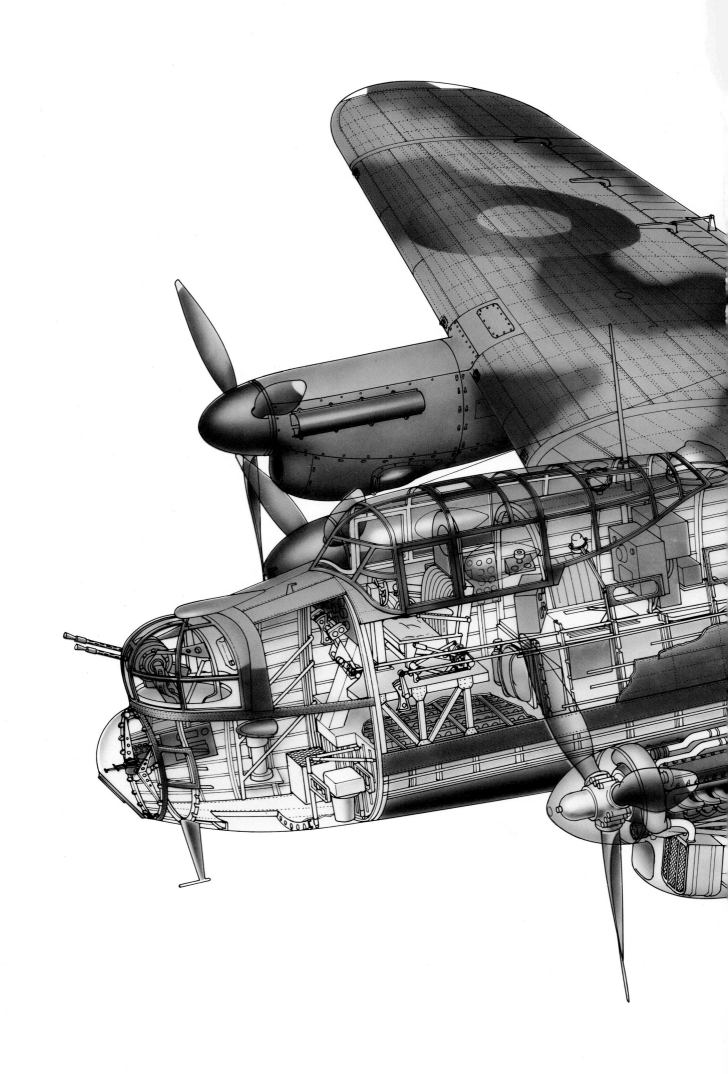

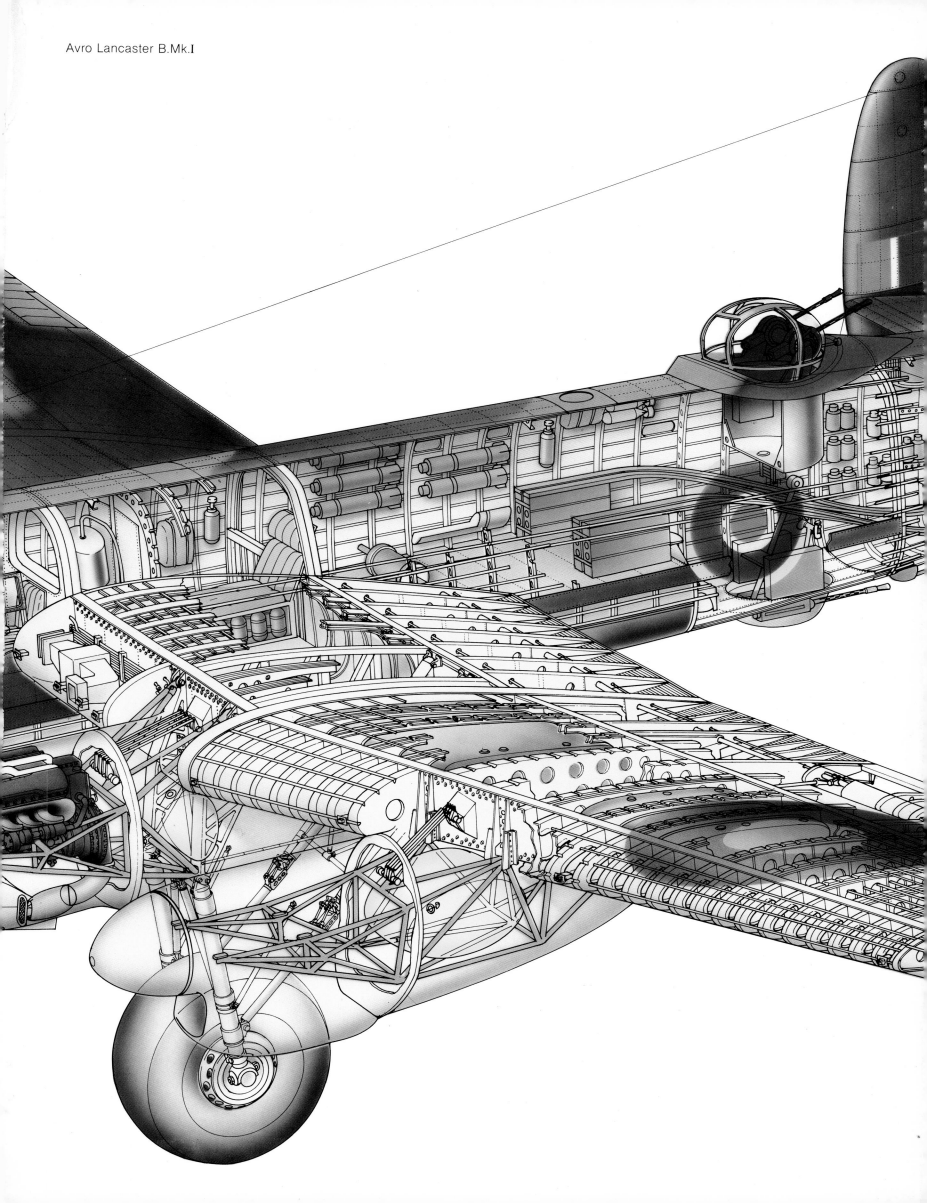

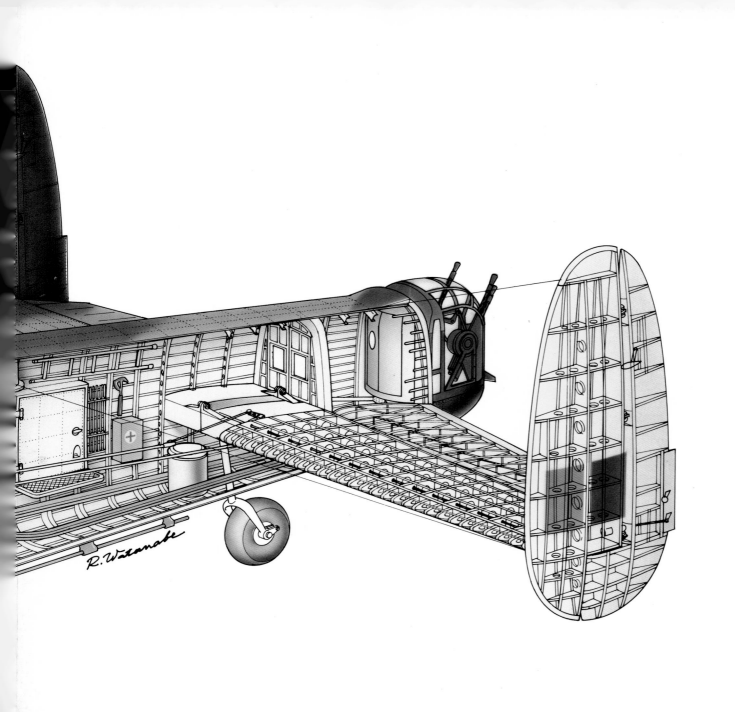

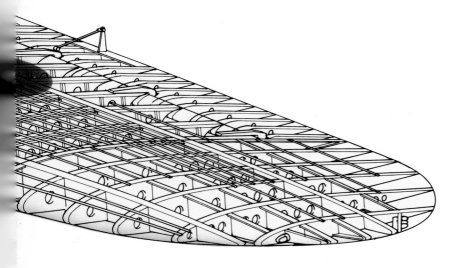

The first Lancaster prototype as originally flown, retaining the Manchester's small span tailplane and triple fins.

The Manchester I had not quite ended its career, however. In July 1941 a number of aircraft with fully modified cooling systems were flown for 15 hours a day by the squadrons. By August, seven units were equipped with Manchesters, and by November the type outnumbered the Halifaxes in Bomber Command. But the first production example of the four-engined variant had flown in October 1941 (unlike the first aircraft, it had the later twin-fin tail of the Manchester IA), and in January 1942 a relieved 97 Squadron converted from the Manchester to its descendant. By the time production ended, Avro had delivered 159 Manchester Is and IAs, including the two prototypes, and Metropolitan-Vickers had delivered 43. In June 1942 the type was withdrawn from operations and sent to operational training units, where the last was retired in the following year.

Before production of the Manchester III began, it was decided that in view of the miserable reputation which the Manchester I and IA had earned in service, it would be advisable to reflect the major modification to the aircraft in a new name. The Type 683 became the Lancaster I.

The durable Lancaster

The Lancaster underwent very little fundamental alteration during its production life compared with other wartime aircraft. Detail modifications were legion, but any major modifications proposed were rigorously examined by the Air Staff in the light of the cold calculations behind the British bomber offensive. If they would allow more bombs to be dropped on Germany for a given expenditure of effort they were approved, whether they achieved this aim by increasing production output, increasing the bombload or reducing losses to enemy action. If the cost of any new modification in terms of money or interrupted production could be better spent on simply building more aircraft, the modification was rejected.

The bottom line was the tonnage of explosives and pyrotechnics unloaded on German cities by Bomber Command, and very few major modifications achieved a credit balance sufficient to be implemented during the height of the campaign.

Paradoxically, the number of smaller modifications introduced during the production life of the Lancaster was very large. Any alteration which could be adopted in the field or which would not seriously interrupt production had a good chance of being accepted, and the design of the Lancaster was such that modifications could often be incorporated easily. The result was that the Lancaster fleet, although comprising basically similar aircraft, embraced an enormous range of detail variations.

From the start of flight trials with the production Lancaster I, it became increasingly clear that the tortuous path of development had yielded an aircraft which totally outclassed the similarly powered Halifax. From the beginning it equalled the range and warload of the much heavier Stirling and could attain rather greater altitudes. The Lancaster accordingly replaced the Halifax in plans for production in Canada, and during 1942–43 the Avro bombers started to roll out of Vickers-Armstrongs and Armstrong Whitworth factories as well. Although plans for production by Shorts at Belfast – replacing the Stirling – and in Australia by Government Aircraft Factories never materialised, more than 7,300 Lancasters were built.

The development of the Lancaster was as smooth as might have been expected, considering that both the engine and the airframe were already known quantities. The prototypes were fitted with the Merlin X engine, which was the first subtype to be fitted with a two-speed supercharger drive. It delivered 1,280 hp for take-off, and at altitude the supercharger could be shifted into high gear, increasing the boost pressure, and the engine's output was 1,010 hp at 17,500 ft (5,330 m). The first production aircraft had the Merlin XX rated at 1,390 hp on take-off, and 1,435 hp at 11,000 ft

(3,350 m). All production Lancasters used the same basic Merlin 20 series, with a single-stage, two-speed supercharger. Only the Mark II and a few later Mark VI conversions differed in this respect.

The first few Lancaster Is differed from later aircraft in their fuel system, with standard tankage for 1,710 Imp gal (7,774 lit) in four wing cells; all subsequent aircraft carried 2,154 Imp gal (9,792 lit) in six tanks, and could take-off at 63,000 lb (28,577 kg) all-up weight instead of 61,500 lb (27,896 kg). This was the standard Lancaster I, in all essentials similar to the aircraft being produced at the end of the war.

The only serious technical problems encountered by the Lancaster concerned the structure and the fuel system. Problems with the system of immersed pumps originally installed halved the operational strength of the Lancaster force in autumn 1942, before a series of temporary fixes and permanent modifications cured the difficulties. Another early problem involved failures of the outer wingtip under high load, leading to a brief grounding in March 1942 until the joint could be strengthened. The Lancaster's Achilles heel, however, was its tail unit. Early aircraft were subject to fin failures under high loads (such as evasive manoeuvring) until the fin-tailplane junction was reinforced. Then, in the second half of 1943, nearly a dozen Lancasters were lost on training flights under similar and mysterious circumstances, usually involving uncontrollable high-speed dives. No single cause was ever found for these accidents, and sabotage was suspected at one time, but the most likely theory was that the fabric covering of the elevator may have separated from the ribs because of wear and tear. Pilots were warned not to use the elevator trim tab to assist the entry to a dive, but to keep it in reserve to help the pull-out, and that the engineer should stand by to help the pilot pull the stick back in any long dive. Other than these problems, the Lancaster's record was good, certainly far better than that of the mulish Halifax. The type's loss rate from all causes was consistently the lowest of any of the Bomber Command heavies.

The Lancaster I was the most widely produced version of the type, the vast majority of aircraft being either Lancaster Is or Lancaster IIIs, the latter differing solely in having Packard-built engines and associated changes to engine accessories and controls. The only production version to differ externally from the Merlin-powered types was the Lancaster II. This version, powered by Bristol Hercules VI or XVI radial engines, was developed as an insurance against the failure of the supply of Merlins from the USA. The Avro-built prototype was flown in November 1941. After the USA entered the war the following month it was decided to produce the Lancaster II in quantity, in case the Packard Merlin

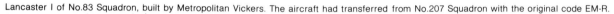

Lancaster I of No.83 Squadron, built by Metropolitan Vickers. The aircraft had transferred from No.207 Squadron with the original code EM-R.   (Imperial War Museum)

production was diverted to the US forces. Three hundred Lancaster IIs were built by Armstrong Whitworth at Baginton, but the altitude performance of the Hercules was not as good as that of the Merlin and the Lancaster II was replaced in production by the basic aircraft. Most of the Lancaster IIs were delivered as standard with ventral gun turrets and enlarged bomb-bay doors.

The Lancaster I and III were operated with a variety of Merlins. The Merlin 22 from Derby and the Packard-built Merlin 28 and 38 had basically the same ratings as the original Merlin XX, but could deliver slightly more power at sea level and were preferred for operations at high weights. Some fortunate squadrons – usually the crack units or those selected for special operations – had the more highly boosted Merlin 24 or 224 (the latter being the American-built engine) rated at 1,610 hp for take-off, 16 per cent more than the normal engines. Some Packard-engined Lancasters had the US-developed large-area "paddle-bladed" propellers, which improved high-altitude performance and climb significantly, but which gave inferior performance below 16,000 ft (4,877 m).

Chadwick's heavy bomber was successful because it was perfectly suited to its intended role. It represented exactly the right balance between effectiveness and cost, and the fact that it did so was in large measure due to the basic design produced by the Avro team.

Lancaster II, powered by four 1,725 hp Bristol Hercules VI radial engines.   (Imperial War Museum)

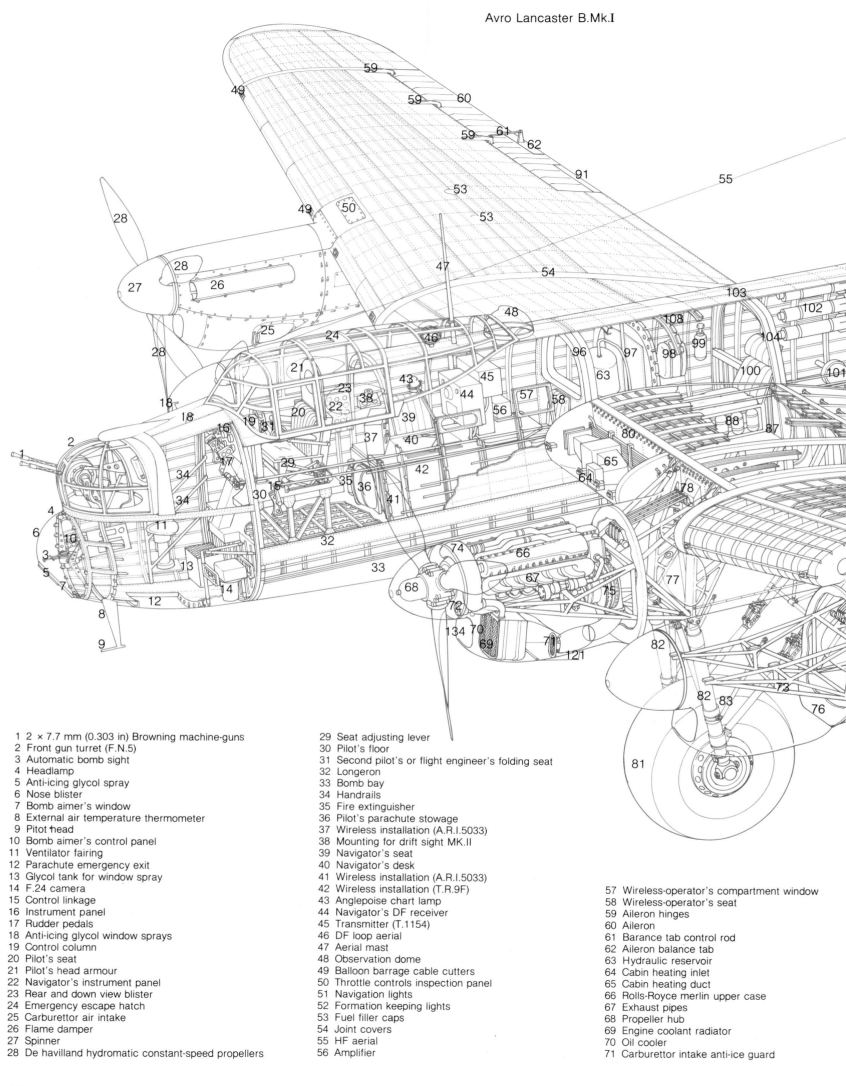

Avro Lancaster B.Mk.I

1 2 × 7.7 mm (0.303 in) Browning machine-guns
2 Front gun turret (F.N.5)
3 Automatic bomb sight
4 Headlamp
5 Anti-icing glycol spray
6 Nose blister
7 Bomb aimer's window
8 External air temperature thermometer
9 Pitot head
10 Bomb aimer's control panel
11 Ventilator fairing
12 Parachute emergency exit
13 Glycol tank for window spray
14 F.24 camera
15 Control linkage
16 Instrument panel
17 Rudder pedals
18 Anti-icing glycol window sprays
19 Control column
20 Pilot's seat
21 Pilot's head armour
22 Navigator's instrument panel
23 Rear and down view blister
24 Emergency escape hatch
25 Carburettor air intake
26 Flame damper
27 Spinner
28 De havilland hydromatic constant-speed propellers

29 Seat adjusting lever
30 Pilot's floor
31 Second pilot's or flight engineer's folding seat
32 Longeron
33 Bomb bay
34 Handrails
35 Fire extinguisher
36 Pilot's parachute stowage
37 Wireless installation (A.R.I.5033)
38 Mounting for drift sight MK.II
39 Navigator's seat
40 Navigator's desk
41 Wireless installation (A.R.I.5033)
42 Wireless installation (T.R.9F)
43 Anglepoise chart lamp
44 Navigator's DF receiver
45 Transmitter (T.1154)
46 DF loop aerial
47 Aerial mast
48 Observation dome
49 Balloon barrage cable cutters
50 Throttle controls inspection panel
51 Navigation lights
52 Formation keeping lights
53 Fuel filler caps
54 Joint covers
55 HF aerial
56 Amplifier

57 Wireless-operator's compartment window
58 Wireless-operator's seat
59 Aileron hinges
60 Aileron
61 Barance tab control rod
62 Aileron balance tab
63 Hydraulic reservoir
64 Cabin heating inlet
65 Cabin heating duct
66 Rolls-Royce merlin upper case
67 Exhaust pipes
68 Propeller hub
69 Engine coolant radiator
70 Oil cooler
71 Carburettor intake anti-ice guard

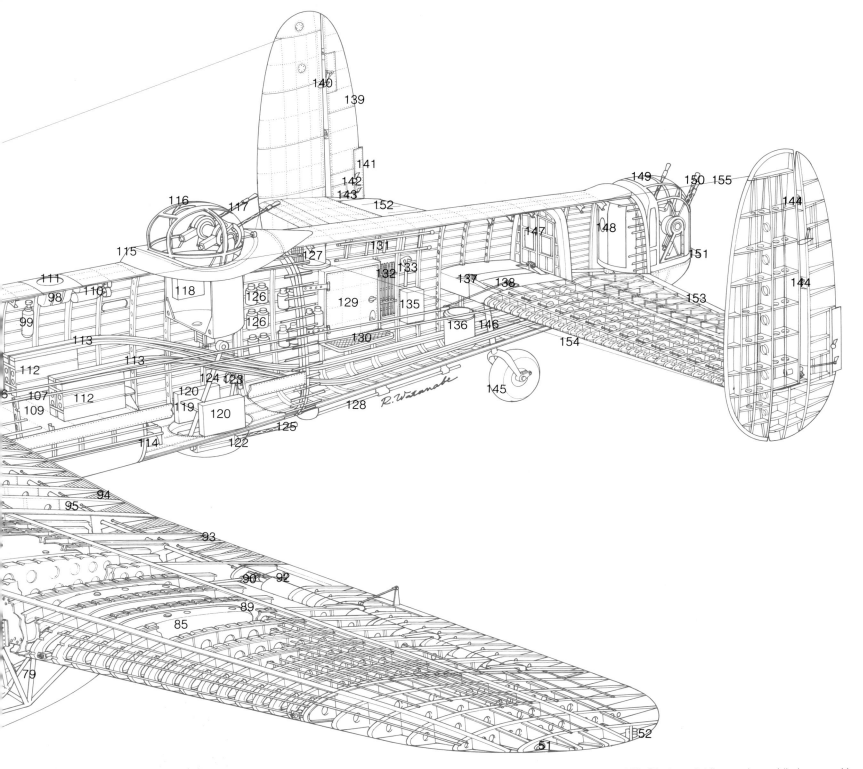

72	De Havilland constant-speed unit on motor casing	
73	Engine support frames	
74	Glycol header tank	
75	Super charger components	
76	Firewall/engine bulkhead	
77	Oil tanks	
78	Throttle controls	
79	Engine sub-frame	
80	Main spar	
81	Main wheel	
82	Main wheel shock-absorber struts	
83	Undercarriage door operating link rod	
84	Undercarriage retraction jack	
85	No.3 fuel tank (518 ltr/114 Imp. gal)	
86	No.2 fuel tank (1,741 ltr/383 Imp. gal)	
87	No.1 fuel tank (2,637 ltr/580 Imp. gal) position	
88	Oxygen bottles stowage (15 bottles)	
89	Rear spar	
90	Aileron control	
91	Aileron trim tab	
92	Trim tab control rod	
93	Outboard split flap	
94	Inboard split flap	
95	Flap operating tube	
96	Spar flange reinforcement	
97	Armoured doors	
98	Parachute stowages	
99	Portable oxygen stwages	
100	Rest bed	
101	Flap jack	
102	Reconnaisance flares	
103	Fuselage joint	
104	Rear spar fuselage frame	
105	Flare chute extension (stowed and in position)	
106	Rudder control cable	
107	Elevator control cable	
108	Windows	
109	Main floor	
110	Sea markers and flame floats	
111	Emergency exit	
112	Tail turret ammunition boxes	
113	Ammunition ducts	
114	Flare chute	
115	Dorsal turret fairing	
116	Upper mid turret (F.N.50)	
117	2 × 7.7 mm (0.303 in) Browning machine-guns	
118	Upper turret ammunition box	
119	Lower mid gunner's seat	
120	Lower turret ammunition boxes	
121	Control shutter	
122	Lower mid turret (F.N.64)	
123	Lower turret control fitted with firing button	
124	Gun control (up and down) arm	
125	2 × 7.7 mm (0.303 in) Browning machine-guns	
126	Vacuum flasks	
127	DR compass housing	
128	Dipole aerial (Lorenz beam blind approach)	
129	Crew entry door	
130	Step over ammunition ducts	
131	Ladder	
132	Dipsticks stowage	
133	Crash axe	
134	Air intake	
135	First aid kit	
136	Elsan closet	
137	Tailplane joints	
138	Rudder control lever	
139	Rudder	
140	Rudder balance weight	
141	Rudder trim tab	
142	Rudder tab balance weight	
143	Rudder tab actuation rod	
144	Datum hinges	
145	Fixed tail wheel	
146	Tail wheel shock-absorber strut	
147	Draught proof doors	
148	Tail turret entry door	
149	Tail turret (F.N.20)	
150	4 × 7.7 mm (0.303 in) Browning machine-guns	
151	Cartridge case ejection shute	
152	Elevator	
153	Elevator trim tab	
154	Aerial for A.R.I.5033	
155	Aerial for navigator's DF receiver and T.F.9	

The Lancaster differed from the Stirling and Halifax in carrying all its bombs in the fuselage, shunning the use of small bomb cells in the inner wing. The massive, uninterrupted, constant-section bomb-bay was the heart of the design, and the reason why the Lancaster could carry a bigger bomb than any other wartime aircraft. Around this bomb-bay, the aircraft was put together in a manner reminiscent of a DC-3 or other Northrop-inspired design, with the centre-section of the wing built integral with the centre fuselage and carrying the outer panels. The outer wings were secured by bolts, pins and shackles to the centre-section, therefore it had not been too hard for Chadwick's team first to increase the span of the Manchester prototype and then to attach the new outer wings of the Lancaster. Simple curved wingtips completed the planform. Thanks to its basis in the much shorter wing of the original Manchester, together with the absence of wing bomb cells, the Lancaster's wing was unusually slender and thin for a British aircraft of the period, and this may have been the secret of its high performance.

Like the wing, the fuselage was designed in large independent sections held together by bolted joints, immensely facilitating repair. Damaged components could be removed rapidly and replaced by relatively unskilled crews. The comparative ease with which the major sub-assemblies could be handled was a major convenience in production, and Avro took full advantage of this by ensuring that as much equipment as possible was installed before the components arrived on the final assembly line.

One of the Lancaster's descendants was defined as "20,000 rivets flying in close formation", and this somewhat unkind phrase reflects the Lancaster's structure quite neatly. Instead of using sophisticated machining techniques, most of the Lancaster was built up from basic components joined by riveting. The main exceptions to this philosophy were a number of high-strength aluminium extrusions, including the booms of the front and rear spars and the highly stressed longerons at the top of the bomb-bay. The spars were built up from these extrusions, riveted to a web of Alclad sheet. The structural heart of the fuselage, firmly bolted to the wing spars, was a heavily ribbed double-skinned floor which carried the fuselage loads and the weight of the bombload.

Simplicity of structure was allied to labour-intensive production. The workforce in the Avro manufacturing group, not including Metropolitan-Vickers (although the latter's aircraft were assembled at Avro's workshop) rose from 10,000 in mid-1939 to 23,500 in 1941, and peaked at over 40,000 in 1943–45. The average working week was more than 66 hours, and 44 per cent of the workers were

British general purpose bomb

500 lb (227 kg) MC
Used by RAF in the early years of WWII

1 Tail unit
2 Explosive (Amatol)
3 Nose bushing
4 Locking screw
5 Exploder containers
6 Suspension lug
7 Tail bushing

German general purpose bomb

250 kg (551 lb) SC 250
Used by Luftwaffe through WWII

1 Brace
2 Tail fin
3 After fuze pocket
4 Suspension lug
5 Forward fuze pocket
6 Explosive (Amatol and TNT)
7 Suspension

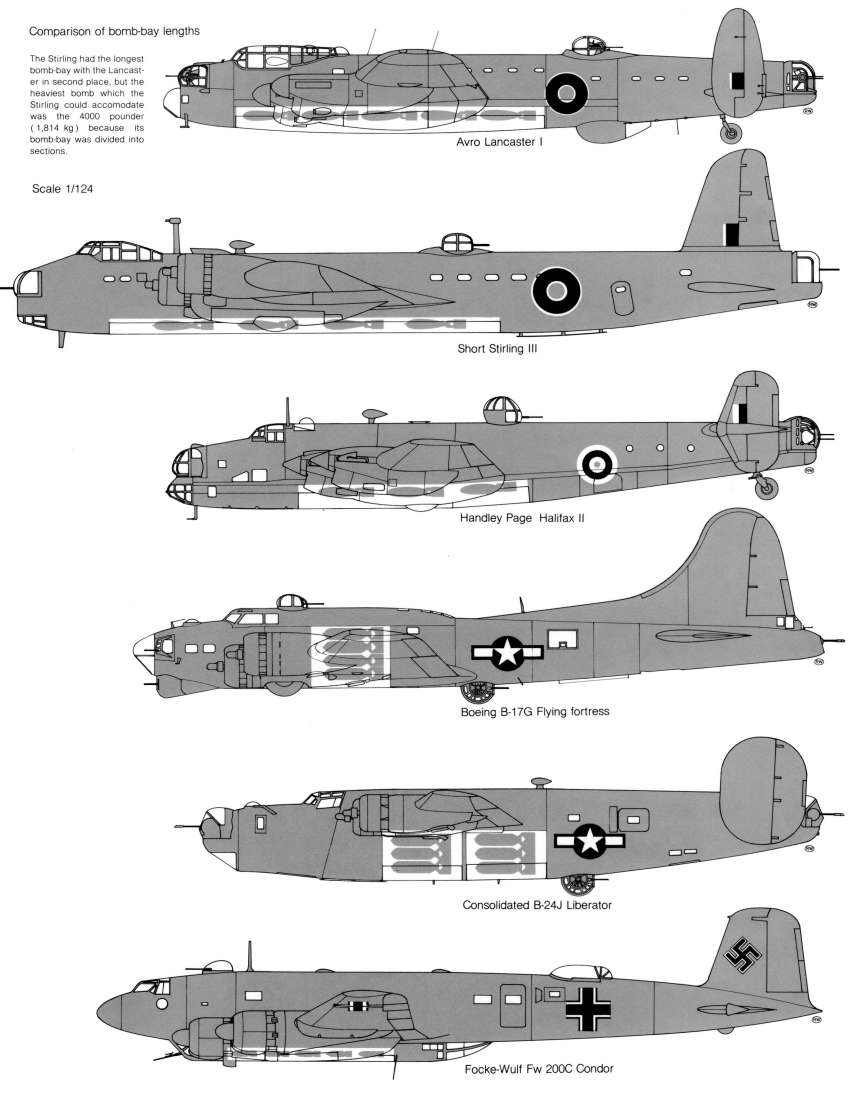

Comparison of bomb-bay lengths

The Stirling had the longest bomb-bay with the Lancaster in second place, but the heaviest bomb which the Stirling could accomodate was the 4000 pounder (1,814 kg) because its bomb-bay was divided into sections.

Scale 1/124

Avro Lancaster I

Short Stirling III

Handley Page Halifax II

Boeing B-17G Flying fortress

Consolidated B-24J Liberator

Focke-Wulf Fw 200C Condor

Avro Lancaster B.Mk.I

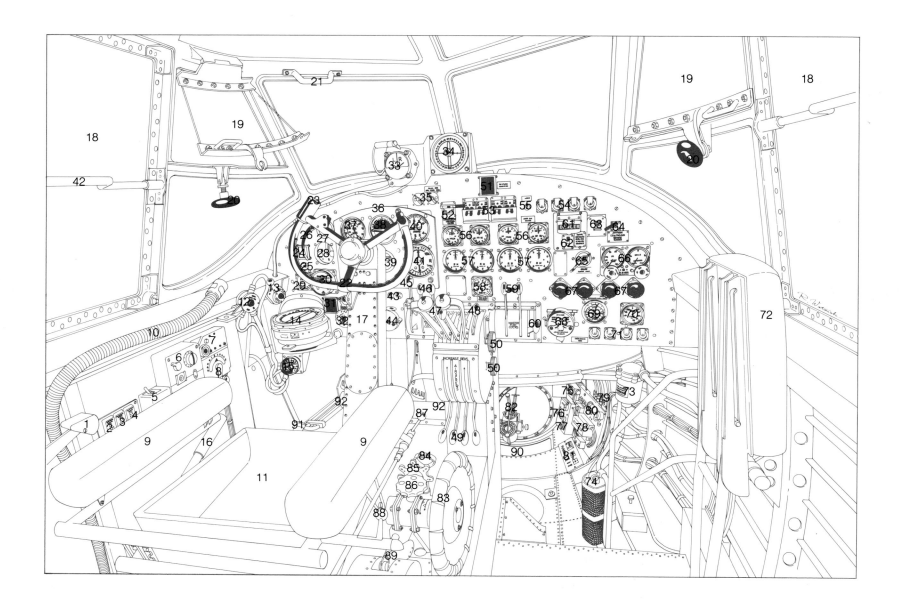

Avro Lancaster B.Mk.I

1 Bomb-bay door control lever
2 Navigation-light switch
3 T.R.9 switch
4 Autopilot master switch
5 Mixer box
6 Beam-approach control unit
7 Intercom call light
8 Autopilot altitude control
9 Folding armrests
10 Oxygen connection
11 Pilot's seat
12 Autopilot lock
13 Autopilot
14 P.4 magnetic compass
15 Autopilot pressure gauge
16 Seat-raising lever
17 Control column
18 Sliding windows
19 Direct-vision windows
20 Window catches
21 Hand grip
22 Control wheel
23 Bomb-release button
24 A.S.I. correction card holder
25 Flap indicator switch
26 Brake lever
27 Watch holder

28 Beam-approach visual indicator
29 Flap indicator
30 Undercarriage indicator
31 P.4 compass-deviation card holder
32 Autopilot speed and heading levers
33 D.F. indicator
34 D.R. repeater compass
35 Landing-light switches
36 Instrument-flying panel
37 A.S.I.
38 Artificial horizon
39 Direction indicator
40 Rate of climb/descent indicator
41 Turn-and-flip indicator
42 Sliding-window hand grips
43 Identification-light colour selector switches
44 Recognition-light signalling switchbox
45 Boost-control cut-out
46 Port master engine fuel-control cocks
47 Throttle levers
48 Mixture lever
49 Propeller pitch controls
50 Friction adjusters
51 D.R. compass-deviation card holder
52 Undercarriage indicator switch
53 Ignition switches
54 Engine-starting pushbuttons
55 Booster coil switch
56 Boost gauges
57 Engine speed (r.p.m.) indicators
58 Steering indicator
59 Starboard master engine fuel-control cocks

60 Two-speed supercharger control
61 I.F.F. detonator buttons
62 I.F.F. switch
63 Bomb-container jettison button
64 Bomb jettison control
65 Vacuum change-over cock
66 Oxygen regulator gauges
67 Propeller Feathering switches
68 Identification-light signalling switchbox
69 Brake pressure gauge
70 Air temperature gauge
71 Fire-extinguisher pushbuttons
72 Folded flight engineer's seat
73 Oil transfer pump
74 Oil filter
75 Bomb selector switches
76 Stick-bombing trim device
77 Bomb-interval trimming dial
78 Bomb-dropping selector box
79 Master switch
80 Camera controls
81 Automatic bombsight
83 Elevator trim-tab control
84 Flap control
85 Aileron trim-tab control
86 Rudder trim-tab control
87 Pilot's harness-release lever
88 Undercarriage-control safety bolt
89 Undercarriage control
90 Emergency exit
91 Pilot's microphone socket
92 Rudder pedals

women. Only a small proportion of the staff had more than a couple of years' experience of aircraft production. Maximum output, attained in August 1944, was 155 Lancasters a month. This was equivalent to something like 2.5 man-hours per pound of airframe empty weight, whereas modern airliners take rather less than one man-hour per pound weight. But the predominantly riveted structure could be produced easily and reliably by people with little training, with minimal need for costly tooling and machinery.

Contributing to the ease of maintenance and repair which characterised the Lancaster was the "power egg" concept, applied for the first time to the heavy bombers. The engine, cooling system and all other accessories were installed as a single unit, with control lines going in and electrical, hydraulic and pneumatic power for the aircraft systems coming out. The engines were mounted in cradles cantilevered from the wing, slightly below the chord line. Chadwick's design of the inner engine mount was particularly ingenious – a pair of forged members attached to the front spar not only took the loads from the engine but carried the main undercarriage pivots on their lower ends. The front and rear spars were fitted with attachment points for a specially designed gantry for engine removal and replacement.

By 1941 standards, a heavy bomber was a complex aircraft, but in comparison with modern aircraft the Lancaster was relatively simple. The simple split flaps, for example, were operated by a single hydraulic jack, the sections being connected with torque tubes. The main hydraulic system – operating the landing gear, flaps and bomb doors – was fed from pumps on the inboard engines, as were the pneumatic brakes and the electrical system. A Lancaster could therefore lose either inboard engine and continue functioning, and there was an emergency compressed-air system for the landing gear and flaps.

The "standard" Lancaster as defined by the official manual had a defensive armament of ten 0.303 in (7.7 mm) Colt-Browning machine-guns, mounted in twin-gun Frazer-Nash turrets in the nose, dorsal and belly positions, and a four-gun turret in the tail. The tail gun was provided with nearly twice as much ammunition as the rest of the turrets put together. The majority of Lancasters, however, lacked a ventral turret, and this created a dangerous blind spot which the Luftwaffe would later exploit. A Lancaster with its full design complement of ten guns would have a crew of eight, but the more common three-turret aircraft carried seven men.

Captain of the aircraft, irrespective of rank, was the pilot. Originally designed to be flown by a pilot and co-pilot, the Lancaster was used operationally with a single pilot and a flight engineer. This crewing system had been introduced by the RAF as the Lancaster entered service to reduce the demand for pilots, but placed a heavy strain on the captain – he was not only in charge of the aircraft but had no qualified relief at the controls. The Lancaster was equipped with a Mk IV automatic pilot, consisting of three air-driven gyroscopes linked to pneumatic servo motors. The servos drove the controls via chain drives. The system was powered by an air compressor on the port inboard engine and could, in theory,

Above: Nose mounted F.N.5 turret on a Lancaster B.Mk.III. The aerials on either side are for the Rebecca blind approach landing system. (Imperial War Museum)

Below: F.N.20 tail turret. Many gunners removed the perspex panel as here for greater visibility. (Imperial War Museum)

hold the aircraft straight and level with one outboard engine stopped and feathered. The autopilot could not be used over enemy territory, because disengagement of the autopilot could cause a fatal delay in taking evasive action under attack. There were no Lancaster trainers, but dual-control kits could be fitted.

Behind the pilot was the Lancaster's administrative office, containing the navigator and wireless operator. Originally a somewhat bare and cavernous space in the early Lancasters, by the end of the war this area was to contain equipment totally undreamt of when Chadwick mapped out the Lancaster's crew compartment in 1936. The bomb-aimer lay prone in the nose for the run into the target, his head projecting into a perspex dome. He could also man the front turret. The crew complement comprised the mid-upper gunner, his feet dangling into the rear fuselage (where the ventral gunner's head would be in a four-turret Lancaster) and, last, coldest, but often the most important, "Tail-End Charlie", the rear gunner. All the turrets except the rear guns included their own ammunition supply, but the 10,000-round tanks for the rear turret were located near the end of the bomb-bay and fed the guns via long steel chutes which snaked towards the tail. The Lancaster's armour protection consisted of a bulkhead across the centre fuselage, ahead of the mid-gun positions, with some armour around the pilot. The standard escape routine, even for the tail gunner, was for all the crew to leave by the escape hatch provided under the nose – use of the normal entrance door was cautioned against because of the risk of striking the tail. Only just over a tenth of Lancaster crewmen survived if their aircraft were destroyed by enemy action.

The Lancaster was an aircraft of few vices, and could be thrown around very violently in the "corkscrew" evasive manoeuvre practised by Bomber Command. A determined corkscrew was a test of the aeroplane itself and the pilot – a sequence of wingover, maximum-rate descent and climbing turn in which vertical and horizontal airspeed and attitude fluctuated wildly to the maximum permissible values. The aircraft was restricted to straight and level flight at the higher operational weights introduced later in its life, but would usually have burned off sufficient fuel to be free of restrictions over enemy territory. However, only the Merlin 24 and 224 were really powerful enough to restore the Lancaster's initial climb performance at the gross weights of up to 68,000 lb (30,850 kg) that were used on some long-range missions towards the end of the war, and the more powerful engines were relatively scarce.

The standard Lancaster had been designed to accept bombs as big as the 4,000 lb (1,815 kg) "cookie" thin-cased bomb but many aircraft were built or field-converted with larger bomb doors to accommodate the 8,000 lb (3,630 kg) "blockbuster" or the larger 12,000 lb (5,445 kg) demolition bomb, the former being introduced in 1943 and the latter in 1944. Defensively, the possibility of using heavier guns than the relatively ineffective 0.303 in (7.7 mm) Colt-Browning had been considered in the Air Staff's 1938 "ideal bomber" paper. However the supply of the obvious substitute, the American 0.5 in (12.7 mm) machine-gun, was never sufficient to allow change on any large scale before 1944, when some Lancaster Is and IIIs were fitted with Frazer-Nash FN.82 or Rose Brothers tail turrets, mounting two of the American weapons. When Austin Motors became the last company to commence Lancaster production it was intended to produce a new version, the B.VII, with 0.5 in guns in the dorsal and tail turrets, the former being moved further forward than on earlier versions. The shortage of heavier guns led to some aircraft being completed as B.I (Interim) types with the existing turrets in the new position, but a few B.VIIs were completed before the end of the war.

The advanced Merlin with two-stage supercharger was never used in significant numbers on the Lancaster. The Lancaster IV and V, extensively redesigned to take full advantage of the new Merlin's high-altitude performance, became the post-war Lincoln – Bomber Command's constant demands for more Lancasters prevented the Lincoln from being produced any earlier. Rolls-Royce fitted the two-stage Merlin 85 to a few Lancasters. These, designated Lancaster VI, were used by 635 Squadron for electronic-counter-measures work. Externally the standard production Lancaster remained very much the same throughout its career, although internal changes were many and vital. Despite the enthusiasm with which 44 Squadron at Waddington received their new aircraft in December 1941, the Lancaster B.I was then virtually useless as a weapon system. The story of its increasing effectiveness reflects the campaign of Bomber Command from 1942–45.

Bombing blind

It was not Roy Chadwick's fault that the Lancaster was ineffective, and neither could the blame be laid at Rolls-Royce's door – it was simply that the Lancaster was unable to defend itself in daylight and unable to find its targets at night. This was because the pre-war proponents of bombing had believed, like those who called for the bomber to be outlawed, that the effects of bombing would be far more devastating than they actually were.

The pre-war staff of Bomber Command considered that they alone presented a workable alternative to the terrible trench warfare of the 1914–18 war. Their aim was to build up a bomber force which would realise for its victims the most nightmarish fantasies of the early 1930s. The attitude of the bomber enthusiasts towards the practitioners of more traditional forms of warfare could, on occasion, slip over into

Canadian-built Lancaster B.Mk.X with extended bomb-bay to carry the 8,000 lb (3.629 kg) bomb. This plane was used for trials of Martin dorsal turret (two 0.50 in/12.7 mm guns) which is shown just after the bomb-bay doors. (Imperial War Museum)

open contempt. A staff Group Captain noted to the Chief of the Air Staff in September 1936 that he anticipated that the War Office would, in time of war, experience "natural difficulties" in finding "sufficient morons willing to be sacrificed in a mud war in Flanders". The author of this memorandum was Group Captain Arthur Harris, of whom we will hear rather more later.

Like the advocates of disarmament, Bomber Command believed that an efficient air campaign would cause a rapid and total collapse of civilian morale, and force an enemy to sue for peace. Although there was, at this time, no overt decision to bomb civilian populations, there was little ground for supposing, given the state of the art of the bomber force, that the non-combatant could be effectively spared from damage. The belief of some officers that the attack on the civilian centres should be the primary purposes of bombing was only to be expressed publicly at a later stage of the war.

There were two dangerous and connected fallacies underlying Bomber Command's confidence in its ability to win the war through such a campaign of bombing. The first was the belief that unescorted bombers could survive in daylight against fighter defences by using their multiple guns, mutual fire-support between aircraft and their speed. Even in July 1939 this policy was being questioned by the Commander-in-Chief of the bomber force, Sir Edgar Ludlow-Hewitt. Gunners, he noted, "have no real confidence in their ability to use this equipment [powered turrets] effectively, and captains and crews have little confidence in the ability of the gunners to protect them". These misgivings were well founded, daylight attacks on the German fleet at anchor being badly mauled by German fighters in the last quarter of 1939. Even though some officers blamed the losses on poor formation-keeping and flak rather than fighters – Harris, by January 1940 in command of 5 Group, still

believed after these losses that three bombers in company "considered themselves capable of taking on anything" – the fact that daylight operations were near-suicidal was slowly driven home.

But if the bombers could not attack by day, they would have to go by night, and it was in the art of night bombing that Bomber Command's most gaping deficiencies were exposed. Between 1937 and 1939 no fewer than 478 of the Command's aircraft force-landed after getting lost on training flights over a friendly country spangled with the lights of peacetime. Sir John Slessor, recalling his time as a Group Captain with the Air Staff in the pre-war years, noted that the RAF had no Bomber Development Unit charged solely with improving tactics and methods until 1939, and that the results of bombing trials carried out sporadically in the pre-war years "should have depressed us more than they did". Unless the crew could identify a pin-point on the ground – and over a blacked-out country this would be impossible – the only means of navigation was dead-reckoning based on predicted winds, which could be no more than intelligently guessed at over enemy territory.

Civilian navigators could use radio direction-finding, but these basic beacon aids were easy to jam and there was a high risk of flying a reciprocal heading. Skilled navigators could take a star-shoot, all bombers being fitted with an astrodome for this purpose, but this required long periods of straight, level flying which would be risky in a hostile area. The commander of 3 Group summed the problems up in May 1939, when he stated that without any outside aid, the average crew could only be expected to get within 50 miles (80 km) of the target.

Even if the crews succeeded in finding the target against all odds, the chances of a Bomber Command strike causing any serious or irreparable damage were small. The Mk VII bomb-sight, standard at the outbreak of war, was more

Lancaster I of No.1661 Conversion Unit, flying over heavy clouds.

(Imperial War Museum)

suited to the Command's old biplane bombers than to the Lancaster, early examples of which carried the Mk VII. The sight could not take account of banked turns on the run into the target, so the aircraft had to approach straight and level if the bombs were not to go wide. Finally, RAF bombs were of 1914–18 design, and compared with Luftwaffe bombs of the same gross weight contained a smaller quantity of less powerful explosive. Not surprisingly, Bomber Command entered the war initially committed to conserving its forces until the heavy bombers could be brought into service and more advanced tactics developed. Meanwhile, in Slessor's words, the early bomber campaign advanced "under the cloak of a complacent publicity which kept everyone happy" while efforts were made "to build up a force which could do what the optimists imagined was already being done".

This cloak was rudely rent asunder by a report submitted to Prime Minister Churchill by his cabinet staff in August 1941. It was already known that one-third of bomber crews returned without claiming to have found the target, and it was found that of the remainder, only one in three had bombed within five miles of the aiming point. This report coincided with an appeal by the RAF for a massive increase in bomber production, to the point where Bomber Command could deploy 4,000 heavy bombers. This would have meant virtually the entire output of British war production being devoted to the manufacture of heavy bombers. The Bomber Command enthusiasts wanted to defeat Germany by bombing to the point where an invasion could land unopposed, but in the aftermath of the report to Churchill they were unlikely to win approval for this plan. Bombing continued to enjoy high priority, but henceforth there would be constant tension between the leadership of Bomber Command, who believed that any effort not put into bombers was wasted, and the supreme leadership of the Royal Air Force and the Allied war effort in general.

The Lancaster entered service just as Bomber Command began to overcome some of its more serious deficiencies. By March 1942, when 44 Squadron started experimental minelaying sorties with the new bomber, one-third of Bomber Command's aircraft were equipped with receivers for the new Gee navigation aid. More sophisticated and flexible than the German beam devices used in 1940–41, Gee transmitted two circular patterns of radio pulses and, with the aid of the receiver and a set of special charts, the navigator could find his position with reasonable accuracy. Relatively difficult to jam, Gee was also protected by a series of elaborate deception operations. Although it was not accurate enough for blind bombing, it was good enough for target-finding.

The Lancaster force grew at an increasing pace after a slow start. The 29 Lancasters which took part in the 1,000-bomber raid on Cologne at the end of May 1942 – the first major operation organised by Bomber Command's new commander-in-chief, Sir Arthur Harris – were the largest force of the type to be used up to then. Bomber Command was suffering from a general shortage of aircraft at that time, due to the failure of the Manchester and the slow deliveries of the new heavy bombers, and the Cologne raid was organised by the expedient of milking training and conversion units of every available aircraft.

Bomber Command's policy was to make the crack 5 Group an all-Lancaster unit, and in the second half of 1942 this Group explored the Lancaster's potential. Daylight raids were attempted – the MAN factory in Augsburg, a main source of submarine engines, was attacked by 12 Lancasters from 44 and 97 Squadrons on 17 August. The flight involved a 750 mile (1,200 km) unescorted penetration of enemy territory, and all but one of the Lancasters were destroyed by the defences. On 17 October a shorter-range, low-level raid met with far greater success. Virtually every available Lancaster in 5 Group joined a 94-aircraft raid on the Schneider armaments factory at Le Creusot in Northern France, losing only one of their number.

By the end of 1942 it was confirmed that the Lancaster was far superior to the Halifax or Stirling. It was well on the way to becoming numerically the most important type in the Command, as production increased at Armstrong Whitworth and Metropolitan-Vickers. The Lancaster was to be used in future for all Bomber Command's most demanding missions. In January 1943, as 1 Group started to convert from Wellingtons to the Avro bomber, Lancasters formed the largest single element in a Bomber Command night raid for the first time. In the same month the Lancaster II was first used operationally, by 61 Squadron. On the type's first operation, it was found that the radial-engined bomber could only attain a maximum altitude of 18,400 ft (5,610 m). The career of the Mk II was relatively short.

The effectiveness of the RAF's bombing was improving rapidly. In the summer of 1942 Harris had been forced to create a new force, comprising hand-picked crews, which would be tasked with leading the main force of bombers to the target and "marking" it with pyrotechnic flares. These were the Pathfinders, or 8 Group, and they wielded a range of new electronic devices. Among them were Oboe, a highly accurate marking aid carried on Mosquitos, and Gee equipment operated by skilled navigators. In addition, the Pathfinders were the first unit to use a revolutionary new aid which offered unlimited range (unlike Oboes) and far greater accuracy than Gee. This was H2S, the world's first ground-mapping radar.

H2S had been made possible by a British invention – the high-powered magnetron, which for the first time made feasible the design of powerful radar on very short "centimetric" wavelengths. Development of a "town-finding" air-to-surface radar using the new magnetron proceeded in

A navigator watches GEE indicator unit. (Imperial War Museum)

parallel with advanced night-fighter radar. Despite appeals from the Admiralty for priority in H2S deliveries to be allotted to Coastal Command, the bombers were equipped first with the new aid. Scientific Intelligence had also opposed the early deployment of H2S with Bomber Command, on the grounds that the secret of the magnetron would be lost to the Germans as soon as an H2S-equipped aircraft was shot down, but while almost equally good results could be attained with Gee and Oboe, the urgent requests of the bomber leaders carried the day.

A range of devices designed to weaken the enemy's night-defences was also coming into action in the winter of 1942–43. Tinsel was the code-name for a crude jammer consisting of a microphone in the Lancaster's engine nacelle, connected to the radio. The wireless operator swept the available frequencies, listening for an exchange between a German controller and a night-fighter, and blotted it out with a roar of engine noise. More sophisticated was Monica, a simple radar related to early long-wavelength night-fighter equipment, designed to give an audible warning of any aircraft at close range within a 45° arc to the rear. There were always many of those, however, because the German night-fighters were controlled by a system of sector controls running from Denmark to the Swiss border, and Bomber Command had countered by attempting to saturate a single sector with a "stream" of bombers, flying individually but following roughly the same course. Most of the warnings from Monica were generated by other bombers in the stream.

Another innovation preceded Bomber Command's campaign in the first half of 1943 – the introduction of the Mk XIV bomb-sight. It was gyroscopically stabilised to compensate for aircraft manoeuvres and was linked to a primitive analogue computer which took account of the ballistic behaviour of the bombs being used, the direction and speed of the wind over the target (worked out by specially trained crews called Windfinders) and the aircraft's airspeed and altitude. A vast improvement on the old Mk VII, the Mk XIV began to be introduced from late 1942.

Bomber Command's target was Germany's heavy-industry workforce. Saturation bombing of heavy-industry centres was intended to damage factories, but more importantly it was aimed at the homes, morale and lives of the civilian population. The typical raids up to July 1943 involved around 400 aircraft. Although this force was numerically no larger than the experimental raids of 1941, the increasing use of heavy bombers vastly augmented its destructive power. The first Bomber Command raid on Berlin since 1941 took place on March 1, 1943, and was also distinguished by being the first large raid to be composed entirely of Lancasters. The Ruhr was the focus of the Command's efforts, however, leading the March–July period to be labelled the Battle of the Ruhr. Pathfinders and Oboe, the latter used on a heavy raid for the first time in March, were by that time making their full contribution to improved bombing accuracy.

The early attacks on the Ruhr, carried out against the sector-based German night-interception system known as the Kammhuber Line, delivered a total of 58,000 tons of bombs and incendiaries to German targets. Bomber Command flew 18,506 sorties, losing 872 aircraft (4.7 per cent of those dispatched) to the defences.

The odds against any crew surviving a tour of operations in 1943–44 were unfavourable. It has been calculated that 51 out of 100 crew in an Operational Training Unit at that time would be killed on operations, and another nine killed in crashes. Twelve would survive the destruction of their aircraft to be taken prisoner (sometimes seriously injured) implying that roughly one man in five escaped after an aircraft was hit. Three out of 100 would be injured badly enough to be taken off operations. Statistically, one man among the 100 would survive a crash in enemy territory and find his way back to England without being captured or killed. Less than a quarter – 24 out of 100 – would complete their tour of operations unscathed and at liberty. On the German side, the citizens of the Ruhr reacted as the citizens of London had done under heavy bombing, and the effectiveness of the RAF's campaign was not highly rated by the German leaders. The 4.7 per cent loss rate, however, was only just acceptable to Bomber Command, which feared that morale among its crews might collapse if the loss rate rose above five per cent of its sorties.

Still the campaign continued, because there seemed to be no alternative to the mass night raids. The US Army Air Force was building up to its doomed campaign to carry out precision daylight attacks with unescorted, heavily armed, lightly loaded bombers, but was to be driven from the skies by the Luftwaffe. In May 1943 also, Bomber Command experimented with a different form of attack, in a single raid which earned the Lancaster immense popular fame.

This was the raid on the Moehne, Eder and Sorpe dams by a specially formed 5 Group unit, 617 Squadron. The squadron's Lancasters were modified by the removal of bomb doors and mid-upper turrets and fitted with launching gear for the special mine developed by Barnes Wallis of Vickers – the famous bouncing bomb. The weapon was cylindrical, carried with its axis at right angles to the line of flight, contained 6,600 lb (2,994 kg) of RDX explosive (which had replaced the pre-war Amatol) and weighed 9,250 lb (4,196 kg). The bomb was carried by calipers at its ends, and the Lancaster carried a hydraulic motor in the fuselage to spin the bomb backwards at 500 rpm before launching. Dropped at a carefully set altitude, speed and distance from a dam, the weapon would bounce predictably across the water surface, clearing the torpedo nets with which the dams were protected, and with its residual spin energy would crawl down the face of the dam and explode at a pre-set depth. Avro converted 23 Lancaster IIIs to take the mine, and 19 of these aircraft took part in the attack on May 16–17, 1943. Two of the aircraft aborted, and eight were destroyed, but the Moehne and Eder dams were breached, depriving a large area of hydro-electric power and industrial water supplies, and causing considerable flood damage.

The spectacular dams raid drove home a hard operational lesson – a highly trained force of experienced and proficient pilots had successfully attacked a precision target at night and at low level, but had lost 42 per cent of their number. This was no alternative to nocturnal area bombing.

War in the dark

The weapon system which ushered in the crucial phase of Bomber Command's strategic offensive against Germany had been understood in principle since shortly after the invention of radar, and had been ready for operational use in the first half of 1942. It was then, and remains now, one of the most effective, and certainly the simplest means of confusing a radar system. Now known as chaff, it consists of a cloud of aluminium strips which create a dense fog on the radar screen. It was known to its inventors in Britain as Window.

The use of Window was delayed because of the realisation that it would be equally useful to an enemy, and that operation of the device would inevitably betray it. Unknown to the RAF, the Luftwaffe had independently discovered the use of chaff, and had followed the same course of action, suppressing it in the interests of security. But as bomber losses increased in the summer of 1943, a number of factors were favouring the introduction of Window by the British. It was increasingly unlikely, for example, that the Luftwaffe would ever be in a position to mount an air offensive against Britain on the scale now being carried out by Bomber Command against Germany. Fighter Command was also taking delivery of night-fighters equipped with the new AI.X radar, which had much improved resistance to Window jamming. Finally, it was pressure from Bomber Command to introduce a system that promised to reduce losses which overcame the resistance to the use of Window. It was decided to introduce the new weapon on Operation Gomorrah, the raid on Hamburg on July 24, 1943.

Bomber Command could now field nearly 800 aircraft for a single raid – nine in ten of them were heavy bombers and nearly half the heavies were Lancasters. Hamburg presented an ideal target for H2S, because the coastline gave a clear image on the radar screen. The defenders' radars were a mass of flickering light and random echoes, and the tightly organised German night-fighter system disintegrated. Repeat raids on succeeding nights laid waste to the centre of Hamburg, with the loss of 50,000 lives.

The RAF never repeated the initial surprise of Window, although Bomber Command followed the attack on Hamburg with increasingly devastating attacks on targets successively deeper within Germany. By now, the Halifaxes with their inferior payload and range were being used mainly to carry incendiaries, while the withdrawal from service of the Stirlings with their much lower cruising altitude was only a matter of time.

August 1943 saw two notable and significant raids. The secret base at Peenemunde, where the cream of Germany's aeronautical engineers were working on the Fi 103 and A-4 missiles, was the subject of an attack during which 40 out of the 597 raiders were destroyed by flak and fighters. However, a spoof attack, in which aircraft carrying Window simulated a larger bomber force aimed at Berlin, deceived the night-fighter controllers to such an extent that most of the aircraft bombed successfully before the night-fighters could attack, and the high-priority research centre was heavily

damaged. In the same month, Bomber Command returned to Berlin, suffering 7.2 per cent losses, but this figure broke down into 12.9 per cent for the Stirling, 8.8 per cent for the Halifax and 5.4 per cent for the Lancaster. After these early raids, only Lancasters were used for attacks on Berlin.

The early successes using Window led to a reorganisation of German night-fighter tactics. Initially, the destruction of Hamburg provided the opportunity for Major Hajo Hermann to gain acceptance of his proposal for freelance interception by single-engined fighters. These *Wilde Sau* (wild boar) interceptors achieved some success intercepting and destroying night bombers in the brightly lit area above the target, where searchlights, RAF marker flares and the flames of the city below conspired to turn night into day. They experienced high accident rates, however, and their most important contribution was to point the way to two other Luftwaffe tactics. *Zähme Sau* (tame boar) was the use of radar-equipped night-fighters on the same sort of freelance operations that Hermann had advocated. The fighters were simply vectored towards the bomber stream by ground controllers and left to find their own individual targets. The other main innovation was *Helle Nachtjagd* (bright night-fighting), based on the assumption that good visibility favoured the cannon-armed fighter rather than the bomber. Wherever possible, the sky was illuminated by searchlights on the ground and parachute flares dropped from high-altitude aircraft.

The equipment of the fighter squadrons was also improving, while development of improved versions of the Lancaster remained subordinate to the increasing of production rates. The Messerschmitt Bf 110, with its limited range, was replaced by the Junkers Ju88G, which could follow the bomber stream over a far greater distance and was thus better suited to *Zähme Sau* fighting. More importantly, the new fighters were equipped with *Lichtenstein* SN-2 radar which was far less susceptible to Window jamming. However, perhaps the biggest contribution to the Luftwaffe's recovery from Window jamming was made by Bomber Command itself.

In January 1943, a Pathfinder Stirling carrying H2S was shot down near Rotterdam, and the city's name was used as the German code-name for the revolutionary radar device. In the following month, a Bomber Command aircraft carrying the Monica tail-warning radar was shot down and the equipment was discovered. In addition, Bomber Command crews had persuaded themselves that they could discourage searchlight-control radars from locking onto their aircraft by switching on their identification friend-or-foe (IFF) transponders. There was no foundation whatsoever for this rumour, but Bomber Command nevertheless fitted its aircraft with a "J-switch" to activate the IFF transmitter, in an effort to boost morale. Crews also got into the habit of switching on their H2S radars soon after taking off from Britain.

Bomber Command totally failed to appreciate that in electronic terms every bomber dispatched over Germany in late 1943 was carrying two or three long-range identification lamps. The Luftwaffe was quick to fit its aircraft with systems to detect them. The Ju88s carried the Monica-homer – code-named Flensburg – and the FuG 350 Naxos-Z to

Lancaster B.I RA530 of No 57 Squadron, based at East Kirkby, Lincs, in February 1945. Fitted with H₂S radar. Destroyed in a crash on the night of 20/21 March, 1945.

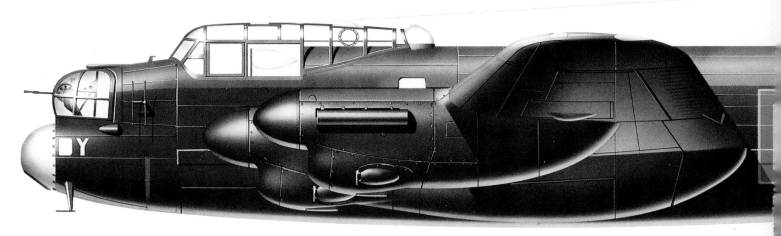

Lancaster B.II DS626 of No 115 Squadron, based at East Wretham, Norfolk, in March 1943. Flown by Sgt G.P. Finnerty (RCAF). Subsequently served with No 426 (RCAF), No 408 Squadron (RCAF) and No 1668 Heavy Conversion Unit. Retired on 20 March, 1945.

Lancaster B.I HK541 modified as experimental long-range bomber for use against Japan. Fitted with 5,460 ltr (1,200 Imp gal) saddle tank. Tested by Aircraft & Armament Experimental Establishment at Boscombe Down in 1945.

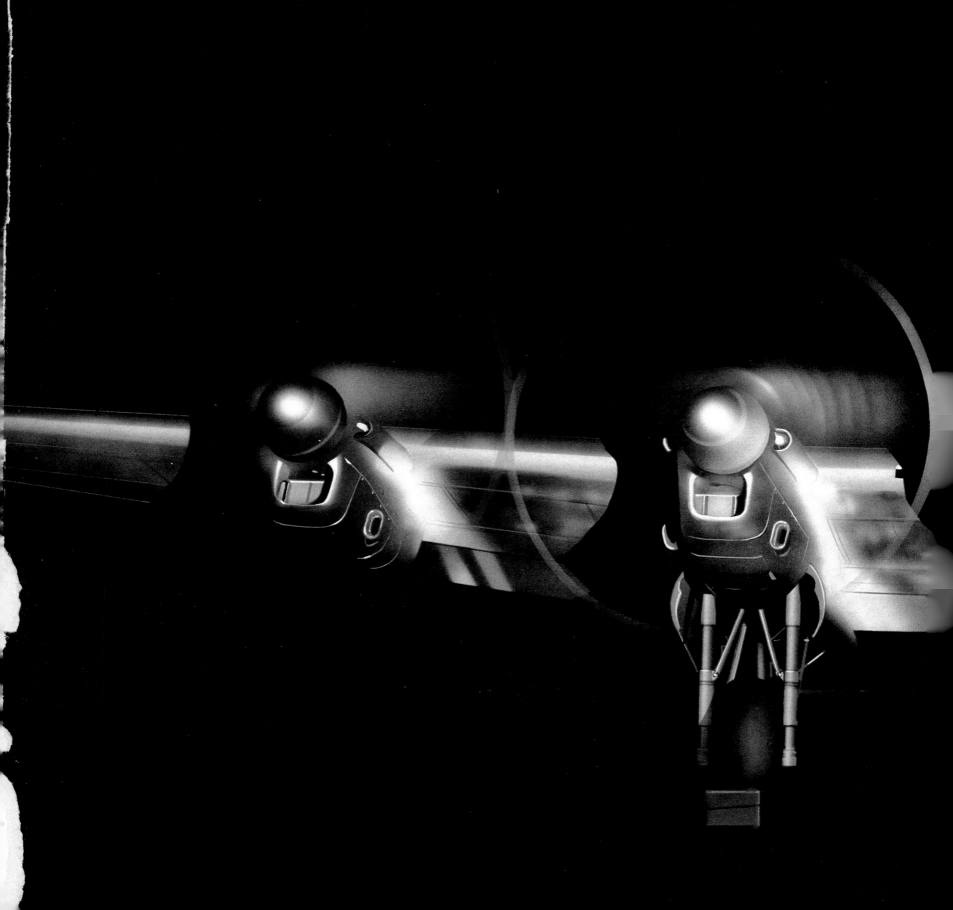

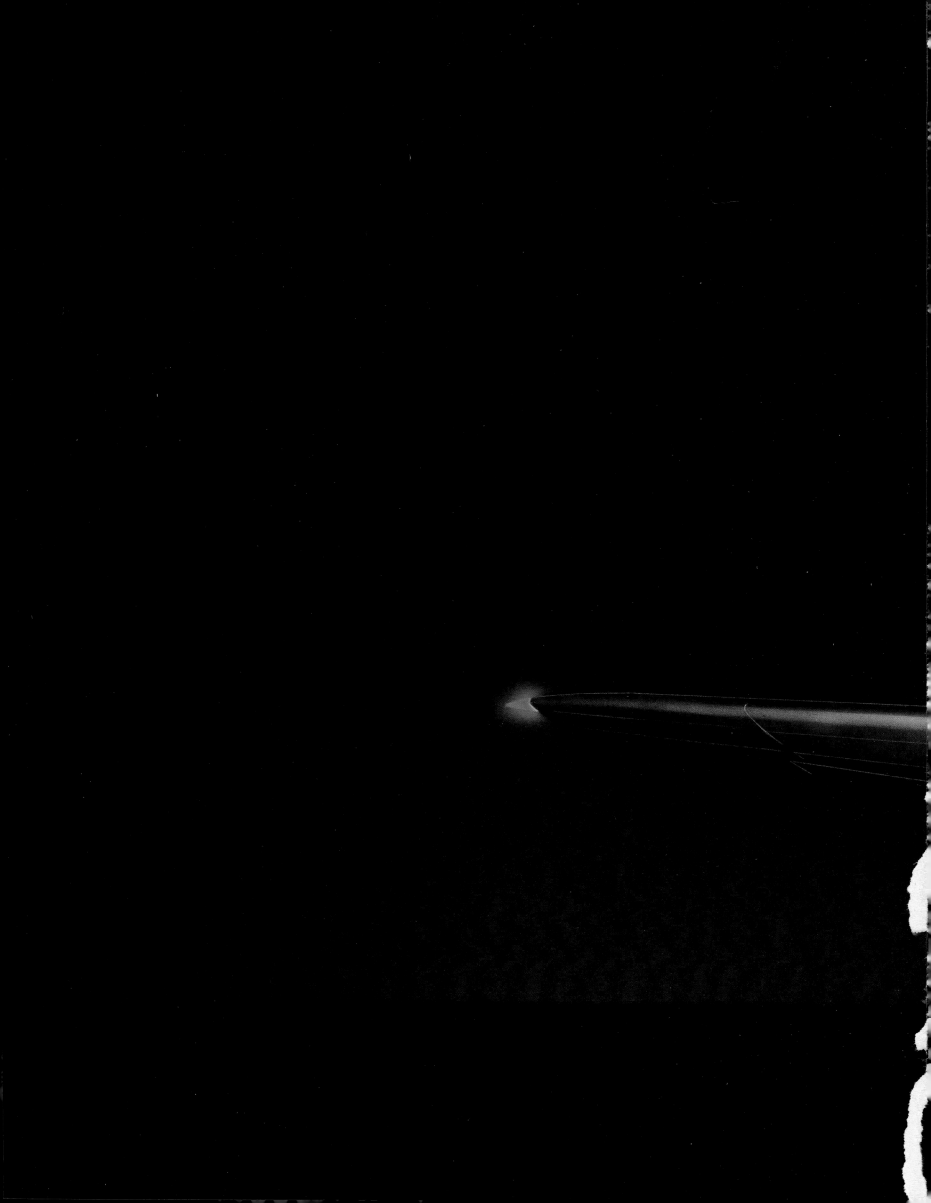

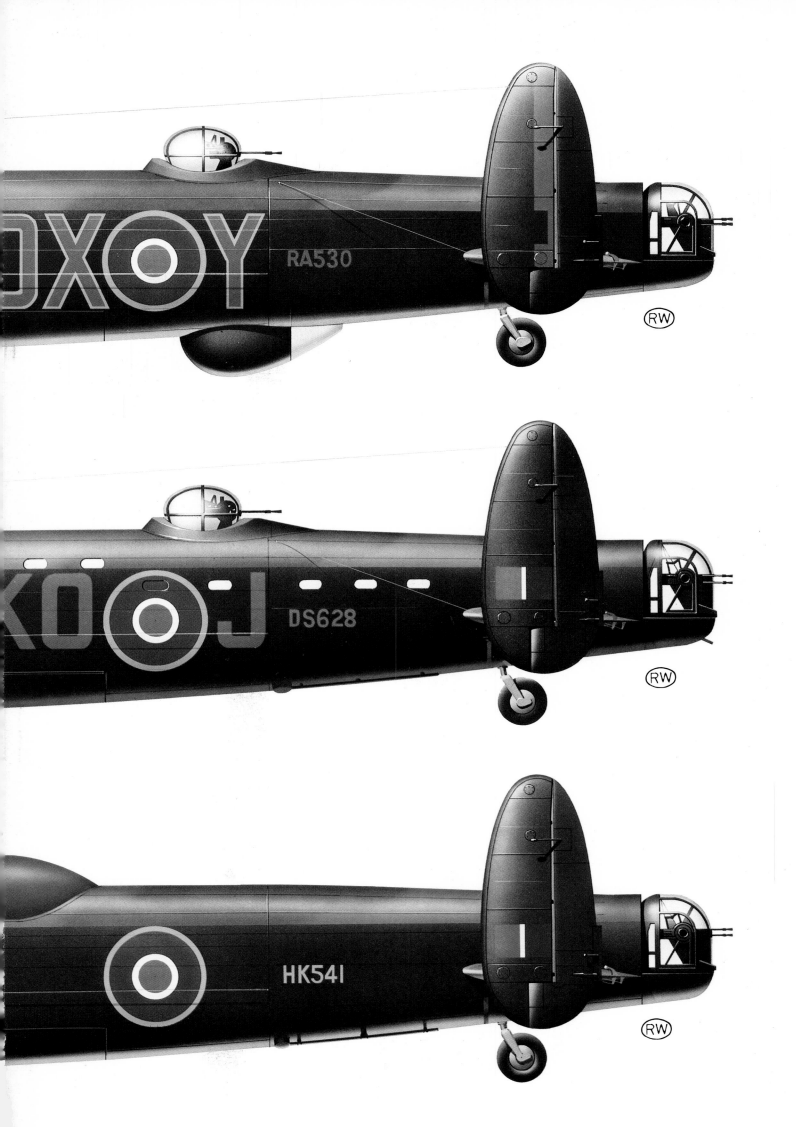

Lancaster B.I (Special) PD131 of No 15 Squadron. Carried 10,000 kg (22,000 lb)
Grand Slam bomb for trials against U-boat pens after the end of the war. Scrapped
in May 1947.

Lancaster ASR.III SW324 with a lifeboat about 1950. Used for rescue duties by No
210 Squadron. Scrapped in May 1957.

Lancaster 10AR KB882 of No 408 (Goose) Squadron, RCAF, at Rockcliffe, Ot-
tawa, in 1963. Used for photographic and Arctic reconnaissance.

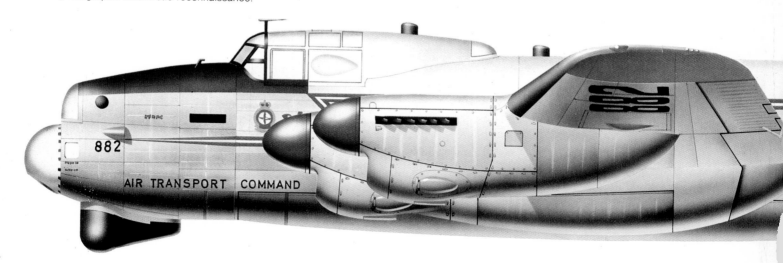

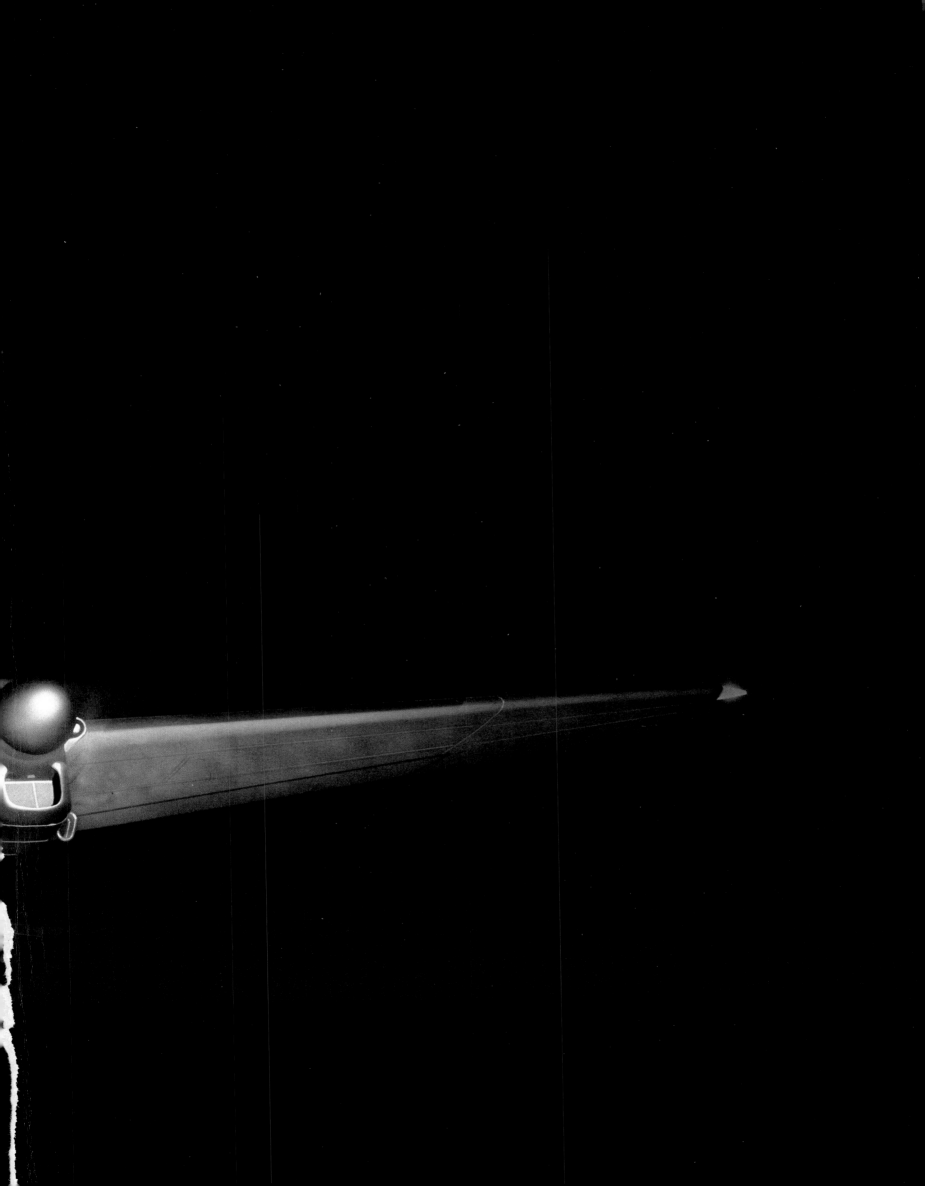

home on H2S emissions. Ground stations were equipped with a combination of both devices, called Naxburg, together with a system which detected the bombers' "flames" or IFF transmissions. Meanwhile, Bomber Command steadily increased the proportion of its fleet equipped with H2S, in either its British version or the American-built H2X, known to the RAF as H2S Mk III and operating on shorter wavelengths.

The German night-fighters were also being equipped with another new device, as simple as it was deadly. This was *Schräge Musik* (jazz music or, literally, "oblique music"), a pair of 20 mm (0.79 in) or 30 mm (1.18 in) cannon installed in the fuselage to fire upwards and forwards. The advantages of this weapon for use against the RAF night bombers were many: the fighter could approach the target from below, reducing its own visibility while silhouetting the victim against the sky; the bomber presented a large target with no deflection required; the fighter could approach without wandering into the cone of detection from the rear turret or Monica radar; and above all the RAF's bombers were almost all completely blind to an attack from below. So lethal was *Schräge Musik* that its existence went unsuspected for many months as victims of an attack did not return to report it and very seldom even escaped into captivity.

It could be argued that the introduction of H2S, which with its ventral scanning aerial was installed on the mounting ring for the original mid-lower turret, was a two-fold menace to the bomber as it supplanted its ventral defensive position and provided the predator with a homing beacon. Throughout the bomber offensive, therefore, some Lancaster units discarded H2S in favour of the ventral guns, particularly the Canadian 6 Group.

There is no conclusive proof of the effectiveness of ventral armament. Many of the Lancasters delivered with the Frazer-Nash FN.64 ventral turret were the lower-flying, more vulnerable Lancaster IIs, so direct comparisons with the I and III would probably be inaccurate. The ventral turret was sighted through a periscope, so the gunner could not fulfil his most effective role, which was that of a lookout rather than an active combatant. The FN.64 was also restricted in traverse to 100° either side of the centre-line. It was probably better than nothing though, and its removal did not make very much difference to the Lancaster's bombload. Also used in small numbers, especially by 6 Group, were simpler ventral defence positions fitted with single manually operated 0.5 in (12.7 mm) or 0.303 in (7.7 mm) machine-guns.

The whole question of the effectiveness of defensive armament was raised in a paper produced in the Operational Research Section of Bomber Command in 1944. Essentially it argued that the defensive armament and gunners were simply heavier and created more drag than they

Lancaster B.Mk.III sets out on a night bombing mission.

(Imperial War Museum)

were worth, and that the speed of the Lancaster could be increased by 50 mph (80 km/hr) by dispensing with guns. Its payload would also be increased, so fewer aircraft would be needed to carry the same tonnage of bombs, the faster aircraft would be less liable to interception, and casualties per aircraft would be lower when they were destroyed. On this question, as on so many other technical matters, it was simply impossible to gather enough data in wartime to present a convincing case for change to the hardline bomber enthusiasts in Command HQ at High Wycombe. There were numerous crews in Britain whose gunners had saved them by driving off an assailant, or more commonly by spotting the attacker in time for evasive action to be effective. Many more crews had found the protection and observation of the gunners inadequate, but often these men were not in Britain – they were in Germany, either in captivity or dead.

While the Luftwaffe improved its night-fighters and bomber development stagnated, Sir Arthur Harris was preparing to launch Bomber Command's biggest offensive. "We can wreck Berlin from end to end," he told Churchill. "It will cost us 400–500 aircraft. It will cost Germany the war." Between November 1943 and March 1944, Bomber Command embarked on a series of raids against major German cities, more than half being against Berlin itself. The Stirlings were withdrawn from raids on Berlin after the second operation, when it became clear that the German defences were too much for them, and the Halifaxes were withdrawn from Berlin a few weeks later.

Harris's appetite for Lancasters was never quite slaked. Victory Aircraft – a consortium of Canadian constructors – completed its first aircraft in August 1943. The Canadian Lancaster X was basically similar to the Lancaster III, with the exception of some Americanised equipment. The aircraft were completed externally, except for their gun tur-

rets, and ferried across the Atlantic for finishing and fitting out. Vickers-Armstrongs completed their first Lancaster in October 1943, the company's Castle Bromwich plant producing 25 aircraft a month by the end of 1944, and the Chester works building 36 a month by the end of the war. This volume of production was necessary because by early 1944, the Lancaster had become a semi-expendable aircraft. The ultimate bomber raids, meeting the fiercest opposition ever from the Luftwaffe, cost more than 1,000 aircraft, twice Harris's estimate.

Losses continued to rise despite the use of specialised jammers such as the Airborne Cigar (ABC) system, a Lancaster modified to jam the night-fighter control, and the similarly intended Corona jamming and deception operations launched from ground transmitters in Britain. Undoubtedly the chief reason for the rising losses was the use of passive homing and the improved SN-2 radar by the Luftwaffe, especially as the new equipment was issued to the best pilots first. By February 1944, the Luftwaffe had 200 SN-2 sets in service, and 28 aircraft equipped with Naxos-Z homers. The RAF's losses rose. At the end of January, 43 out of 683 were lost over Berlin; and in mid-February, 78 out of 823 failed to return from Leipzig. The effect of spoof attacks was variable. It was noted at that time that the German night-fighter system was unstable. If the controllers reported enemy aircraft in a certain spot, the ground observers would hear the approaching Junkers and confirm the report of an attack. This led to some "milk runs" where the losses were in single figures, even in the early part of 1944, but the general trend was upwards and the milk runs were more than offset by the nights where the bombers' luck was out. The last and most infamous of these was Nuremberg, when 94 bombers out of a force of 795 were lost. The bombers' over-use of H2S had been crucial in betraying the nature of a spoof raid towards Kassel – the would-be deceivers were not fitted with H2S.

After the defeat of Nuremberg, the bombers were never again sent to face an unbroken German night-fighter force. In any event, they were needed to prepare the ground for the invasion of Europe, an operation which the Bomber Command enthusiasts had hoped to reduce to a formal occupation of a bomb-wrecked enemy. To that extent the bombers had failed, and there will no doubt be controversy for many years as to the exact degree to which they succeeded. But for the time being, apart from being harried by the Light Night Striking Force Mosquitos, Germany's towns and cities had a period of relief.

The more successful raids had, however, pointed the way to new concepts in bomber tactics, based on subtle electronic systems rather than defensive guns and dead reckoning. More effective developments of H2S would eliminate the problems experienced over Berlin. The city was out of range of Oboe marking, often covered in cloud, and was too widespread to present a clear target to the H2S radar screens. Newer systems would offer better definition. With better training, new bomb-sights and new navigational systems and techniques, Bomber Command was on the point of being able to operate as a precision strike force when the main offensive against Germany was suspended.

Destruction with precision

From April 1944 Bomber Command concentrated on targets directly associated with the forthcoming invasion of Northern France. A series of trial attacks on railway marshalling yards in France in March 1944 had provided startling proof of the RAF's ability to attack precision targets at night without inflicting more than a minimum of damage on the surrounding urban areas. Attacks on the transport system were to receive high priority, although they were ordered with little enthusiasm by the Bomber Command staff. Harris still wanted to organise a full-scale bomber offensive against Germany's industry, and the support of the invasion was incredibly regarded as a distraction.

The most remarkable demonstrations of precision bombing by the Lancaster force were carried out by 617

Squadron, the "dambusters" of May 1943. After the dams raid, 617 was withdrawn from the line to recover from its losses, while 5 Group considered a use for them. No love was lost between 5 Group (which had always considered itself an élite) and 8 Group, the newly formed Pathfinders, and this relationship may have played a part in the decision to use 617 Squadron as the élite precision-bombing unit of 5 Group.

Also influential in this decision was the emergence of a new category of German weapon, the surface-to-surface missile, two of which were under development at the research establishment of Peenemunde. Despite the damage caused by Bomber Command in August 1943, production of the Fi103 cruise missile and the ballistic A-4 continued. In late 1943 it also became apparent that these weapons were to be stored and launched from massive concrete-covered bunkers. Bomber Command was by then using 12,000 lb (5,443 kg) bombs, but these were intended to demolish city houses and were little more than light metal cases filled with explosive. On solid concrete, they would simply shatter. Barnes (later Sir Barnes) Wallis of Vickers-Armstrongs had studied the problem of attack on such installations as part of the process which led to the invention of the spinning mine used on the dams raid in May 1943. Until the advent of the new German missiles his designs had remained in a pigeon-hole at the Air Ministry, but late in 1943 they were taken out again.

Bouncing-bomb spinning mechanism

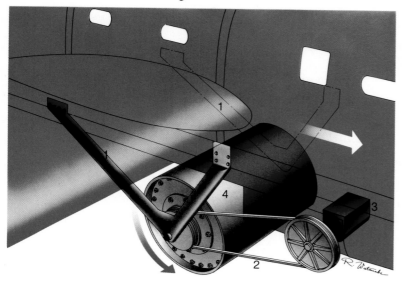

◀ 1 Side arms
2 Driving belt
3 Motor
4 9.250 lb (4,196 kg) bouncing bomb

▼ 1 Lancaster B.III (Special) ED932 "G for George" of No.617 Squadron, flown by Wg. Cdr. Guy P. Gibson flies at a height of 60 ft (18 m)
2 Bouncing-bomb launch
3 Converging searchlight beams indicate precise height for launch
4 Water surface
5 Torpedo nets
6 Net's buoys
7 Dam walls

The attack against Moehne Dam on the night of May 16-17, 1943

Lancaster B.Mk.I in service with No.617 Squadron carrying a 22,000 lb (9,979 kg) "Grand Slam" bomb. (Imperial War Museum)

Wallis's idea was for a heavy, strongly-cased and very streamlined bomb dropped from as high as possible. With a terminal velocity well above the speed of sound, such a bomb would bury itself very deep underground before exploding, creating underground shock waves which would destroy the heaviest structure. The initial version was Tallboy, a 12,030 lb (5,457 kg) weapon, but the ultimate development of the series was Grand Slam, weighing no less than 22,000 lb (9,979 kg).

Vickers-Armstrongs had started to build Tallboys as a private venture in mid-1943, and it was later in the year before the Air Ministry realised that there would be enough targets to justify the procurement of the "earthquake" bombs. Not only were there shelters for missiles, but there were U-Boat and E-Boat pens on the coast and other, more mysterious installations such as that for the V-3 or HDP (from the German initials of its code-name, High-Pressure Pump), a multi-barrel long-range gun. Go-ahead was given for both weapons, Tallboy development running ahead of that of Grand Slam.

Meanwhile, 617 Squadron had been developing the bomb-aiming skills needed to use such expensive weapons effectively. They were helped by the new Stabilised Automatic Bomb Sight (SABS), invented at Farnborough in 1941. Similar in principle to the American Norden sight, SABS incorporated a telescopic sight in which the aimer acquired the target, having fed in the usual information on ballistics, performance and weather. The sight was mounted on a gyro-stabilised platform, and the SABS automatically generated aiming corrections as the aimer held the sight on the target. The drawback was that the aircraft had to make a 20-second straight-and-level aiming run, which was considered unacceptable unless special tactics could be devised and executed by a highly trained unit such as 617 Squadron. Eventually, 617 Squadron could bomb at night with such accuracy that three-quarters of the weapons launched landed within a 75 yd (68.5 m) radius of the aiming point.

Tallboy was first used in action just after the invasion of June 6, 1944, when the weapons were used to block the railway tunnel through which a Panzer Division was due to pass. They were also used to attack the V-weapon launching sites, until the Luftwaffe's loss of air superiority and the increasing weight of the Allies' Operation Crossbow attacks forced the Germans to switch to mobile launching. One of the most important Tallboy operations, however, was the attack on the battleship *Tirpitz* at its anchorage in Tromso fjord, in the north of Norway.

This was a long-range mission for the Lancaster, even with a reduced bombload. To carry the Tallboys to Tromso, the 617 Squadron Lancasters were equipped with extra fuel tanks in the fuselage, and the mid-upper turrets were removed. All the aircraft were fitted with Merlin 24 engines specially overhauled and modified by Rolls-Royce. *Tirpitz* was a relatively small target, well defended by flak and a nearby fighter station, and she had to be attacked in daylight with sufficient surprise to permit bombing before the extensive smokescreens could be activated. An attack plan was formulated with the aid of electronic intelligence "ferret" aircraft, which found a gap in Norwegian radar defences. The Lancasters crossed the coast at low level, breached the airspace of neutral Sweden and flew north, keeping the mountains of Norway between themselves and the radar chain. Crossing into Norway and climbing at the last moment, the bombers took the defences by surprise and wrecked the *Tirpitz* with three Tallboy hits. One Lancaster was lost. The contrast between the *Tirpitz* attack and the early Bomber Command raids over the Schillig Roads and Wilhelmshaven was indescribable – they were a generation of weapons and a revolution in military electronics apart, but were separated by only five years.

When the first Grand Slams were delivered in February 1945, there were few targets worth attention. Production had been delayed by the difficulties of casting the main casing of the massive 25 ft 6 in (7.77 m) weapon. The casing was cast in one piece around a concrete core in a sand mould, and needed special handling equipment even when empty. The Grand Slam bomb was placed in production in Britain and the United States, but 617 was the only squadron to use it operationally, dropping 41 of the weapons on targets such as U-Boat pens. Those at Farge near Bremen were covered with 23 ft (7 m) of solid reinforced concrete, but two direct Grand Slam hits penetrated and wrecked the roof.

Even the Lancaster had to work hard to carry the "special store", the name first used for the Grand Slam and later for other even more destructive weapons. About 30 Lancasters were modified to B.I (Special) configuration, with the nose and mid-upper turrets removed, reinforcement fitted to the bomb-bay, fuselage and undercarriage, and the bomb doors replaced by a fairing into which the Grand Slam was partly recessed. Without the Lancaster, the weapon would have been unusable, but the B.I (Special) could carry the bomb to 20,000 ft (6,100 m) for maximum penetration effect.

For Bomber Command in general, however, the time after the invasion was an opportunity to resume the campaign of bombing against German cities. In July 1944 Harris proposed Operation Thunderclap, aimed directly at the lives and morale of the German population – although it was disapproved in form, Bomber Command largely adhered to it in substance. Only a quarter of the Command's effort was directed against energy supplies, despite the devastating effect this was having on the German war machine and the fact that new navigational devices finally had made such precision attacks possible at night. Bomber Command now threw the bulk of its strength – more than 1,000 Lancasters, over 300 Halifaxes and 200 Mosquitos were available – against Germany's cities, in the Ruhr and elsewhere. Bomber Command's accuracy had improved and its losses plummeted, and the German population was to suffer for it.

Losses were falling largely because of the invasion. The Luftwaffe's early-warning line was being pushed backwards, and the forward bases which the night-fighters could use as they harried the bombers across Western Europe were in Allied hands. By day, even bases well behind the lines were attacked by the Tactical Air Forces, and the aircraft factories were under pressure to build day fighters to protect the troops. The USAAF was back in the daylight skies, with hordes of Mustang and Thunderbolt escorts, destroying the Luftwaffe in the skies and the factories, and wrecking its fuel supplies.

The survival chances of Bomber Command crews were given another boost on July 13, 1944, when a Luftwaffe night-fighter crew committed the classic navigational mistake of taking a reciprocal direction-finding reading and landing their Ju 88G-1 at Woodbridge in Suffolk. Bomber Command realised for the first time the extent to which Monica, the "security-blanket" of the useless J-switch and the excessive use of H2S had been telegraphing the positions of individual bombers over hundreds of miles. Monica was removed and the use of IFF and H2S restricted. Against the weakened German night-fighter force, bombers became safer places. In January 1944 Bomber Command had lost 314 aircraft in 6,278 sorties; by September, when the campaign against German cities was resumed, this fell to 96 losses for 6,428 sorties; and in the following month Bomber Command flew 10,193 missions and lost only 75 aircraft, less than one per cent of the raiders. As losses fell, the numbers and experience of the raiders began to mount.

The Lancaster was also being equipped with a new series of navigation and bomb-aiming devices. Oboe's range had been extended by the invasion, as transmitters were moved further forward, and a new and more accurate version operating on shorter wavelengths was coming into use. More important was a new device known as Gee-H, combining the universal applicability of Gee with near-Oboe levels of accuracy, using a transmitter-receiver in the aircraft to measure distance from ground beacons. Gee-H was introduced by Lancasters of 3 Group in October 1944. Almost simultaneously the K-band H2S Mk VI was introduced, alleviating some of the system's limitations over poorly defined or disguised targets. H2S had been standard equipment on the Lancaster since March 1944.

Bomber Command coupled these new devices with revised tactics. Navigation was now so accurate that decoy fires and spoof raids could be used within a few miles of the actual route. The navigators and bomb-aimers were now

Lancaster B.Mk.I (HK 541) fitted with 1,200 Imp (5.455 ltr) saddle-tank at the Aircraft & Armament Experimental Establishment, Boscombe Down, in the latter half of 1944.   (Imperial War Museum)

Lancaster B.Mk.I Specification

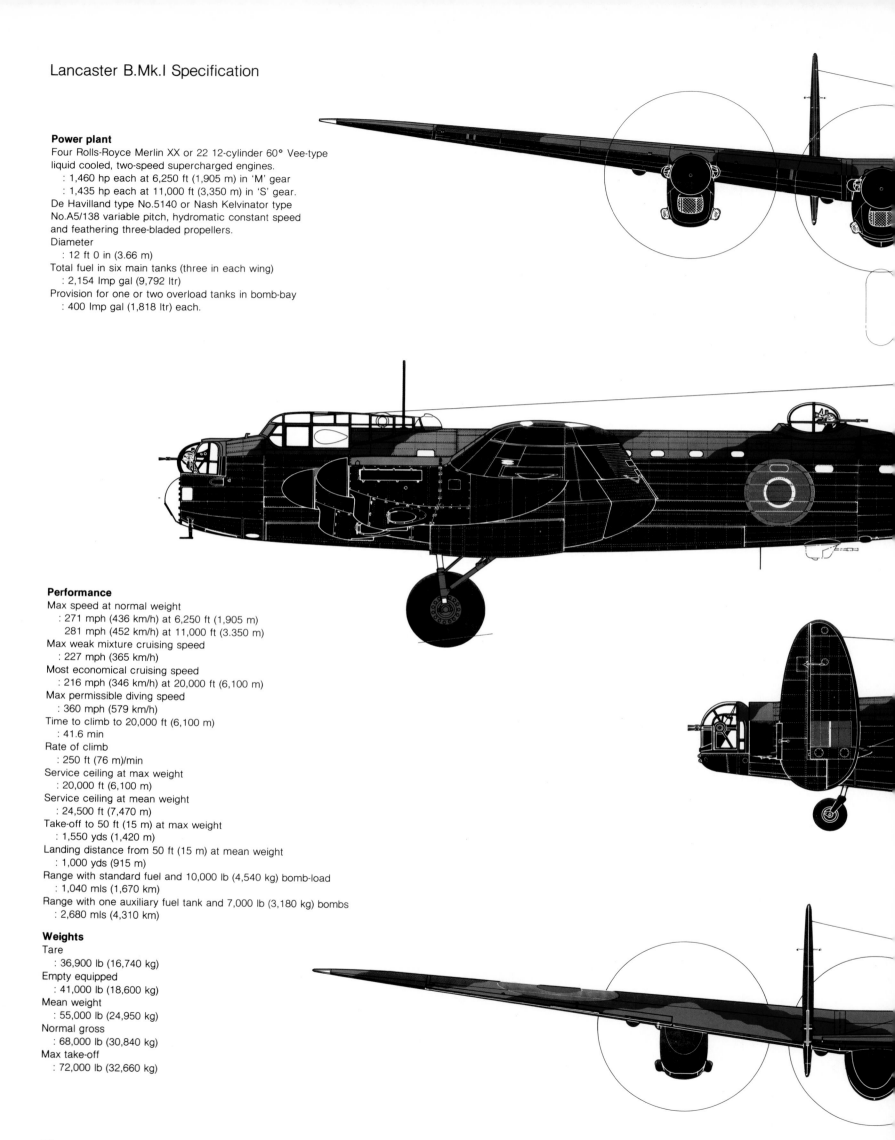

Power plant

Four Rolls-Royce Merlin XX or 22 12-cylinder 60° Vee-type liquid cooled, two-speed supercharged engines.
: 1,460 hp each at 6,250 ft (1,905 m) in 'M' gear
: 1,435 hp each at 11,000 ft (3,350 m) in 'S' gear.
De Havilland type No.5140 or Nash Kelvinator type No.A5/138 variable pitch, hydromatic constant speed and feathering three-bladed propellers.
Diameter
: 12 ft 0 in (3.66 m)
Total fuel in six main tanks (three in each wing)
: 2,154 Imp gal (9,792 ltr)
Provision for one or two overload tanks in bomb-bay
: 400 Imp gal (1,818 ltr) each.

Performance

Max speed at normal weight
: 271 mph (436 km/h) at 6,250 ft (1,905 m)
  281 mph (452 km/h) at 11,000 ft (3.350 m)
Max weak mixture cruising speed
: 227 mph (365 km/h)
Most economical cruising speed
: 216 mph (346 km/h) at 20,000 ft (6,100 m)
Max permissible diving speed
: 360 mph (579 km/h)
Time to climb to 20,000 ft (6,100 m)
: 41.6 min
Rate of climb
: 250 ft (76 m)/min
Service ceiling at max weight
: 20,000 ft (6,100 m)
Service ceiling at mean weight
: 24,500 ft (7,470 m)
Take-off to 50 ft (15 m) at max weight
: 1,550 yds (1,420 m)
Landing distance from 50 ft (15 m) at mean weight
: 1,000 yds (915 m)
Range with standard fuel and 10,000 lb (4,540 kg) bomb-load
: 1,040 mls (1,670 km)
Range with one auxiliary fuel tank and 7,000 lb (3,180 kg) bombs
: 2,680 mls (4,310 km)

Weights

Tare
: 36,900 lb (16,740 kg)
Empty equipped
: 41,000 lb (18,600 kg)
Mean weight
: 55,000 lb (24,950 kg)
Normal gross
: 68,000 lb (30,840 kg)
Max take-off
: 72,000 lb (32,660 kg)

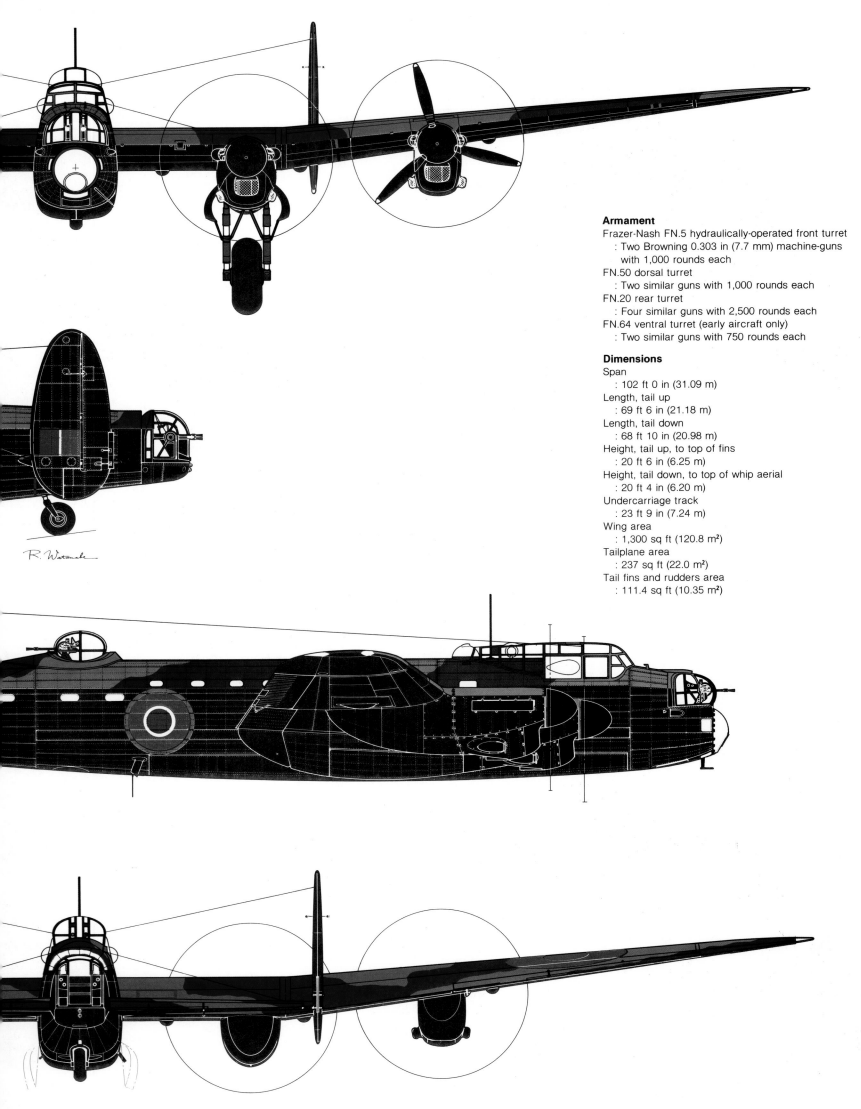

Armament

Frazer-Nash FN.5 hydraulically-operated front turret
 : Two Browning 0.303 in (7.7 mm) machine-guns
 with 1,000 rounds each
FN.50 dorsal turret
 : Two similar guns with 1,000 rounds each
FN.20 rear turret
 : Four similar guns with 2,500 rounds each
FN.64 ventral turret (early aircraft only)
 : Two similar guns with 750 rounds each

Dimensions

Span
 : 102 ft 0 in (31.09 m)
Length, tail up
 : 69 ft 6 in (21.18 m)
Length, tail down
 : 68 ft 10 in (20.98 m)
Height, tail up, to top of fins
 : 20 ft 6 in (6.25 m)
Height, tail down, to top of whip aerial
 : 20 ft 4 in (6.20 m)
Undercarriage track
 : 23 ft 9 in (7.24 m)
Wing area
 : 1,300 sq ft (120.8 m²)
Tailplane area
 : 237 sq ft (22.0 m²)
Tail fins and rudders area
 : 111.4 sq ft (10.35 m²)

R. Watanabe

Bombs

: Fourteen 1,000 lb (454 kg)—14,000 lb (6,350 kg) in all
: One 4,000 lb (1,814 kg) and six 1,500 lb (680 kg) mines—
13,000 lb (5,897 kg) in all
: six 2,000 lb (907 kg) and three 250 lb (113 kg)—
12,750 lb (5,783 kg) in all
: One 12,000 lb (5,443 kg)
: One 8,000 lb (3,623 kg) and six 500 lb (227 kg)—
11,000 lb (4,990 kg) in all
: One 4,000 lb (1,814 kg), six 1,000 lb (454 kg)
and two 250 lb (113 kg)—10,500 lb (4,763 kg)
in all

48

Accommodation
Standard crew of seven comprising pilot, flight engineer
or second pilot, navigator, bomb-aimer/front turret
gunner, wireless operator, dorsal turret gunner and rear
turret gunner.

1   2m

1 2 3 4 5 6 ft

sufficiently skilled to use an offset aiming point chosen for its visibility, and to aim their bombs at a given range and bearing from that point. The raid could also be controlled by a Master Bomber, circling the target and directing the hail of fire and explosive on areas which had escaped earlier waves of the attack. Dresden was just one of the cities levelled in an effort to hasten the end of the war. The technology of destruction by conventional weaponry had reached its peak.

The use of atomic weapons to end the war in Japan abruptly terminated RAF plans to take part in the anticipated conventional bombing and invasion. Under the code-name Tiger Force, a number of options had been considered to enable the RAF to match the range of US aircraft. The conversion of 600 Lancasters to tanker-receivers was planned for mid-1944, but following the successful 617 Squadron raid on the *Tirpitz* it was decided that a standard Lancaster could carry a useful bombload over the necessary range. Also tested, but abandoned, was a Lancaster version with a huge dorsal saddle-tank carrying 1,200 Imp gal (5,455 lit) of fuel, increasing capacity by 50 per cent. The handling of the version was unacceptable and only two saddle-tank conversions were made. Instead, the Lancaster B.I (F.E.) and B.VII (F.E.) were produced by conversions at maintenance units in the first half of 1945. With Merlin 24 engines, no mid-upper turrets and some other equipment removed, but retaining H2S Mk III bombing radars, the aircraft were expected to carry a 10,750 lb (4,877 kg) bombload to Japan from Okinawa. Also included in Tiger Force were the B.I (Special) aircraft of 617 Squadron, intended to use Grand Slam on the bridges connecting Kyushu, where the US forces intended to invade, to the main island of Honshu. Another special version of the Lancaster was the ASR.III, converted by Cunliffe-Owen to carry an airborne lifeboat under the fuselage. Intended to support the raids on Japan, these aircraft became the first Coastal Command Lancasters after Tiger Force was officially disbanded at the end of October 1945.

The Lancaster dropped its last bomb in anger on April 25, 1945, during an operation against submarine fuel stores. After the surrender of Germany, Bomber Command took part in operations to repatriate prisoners and bring the 8th Army back from the Middle East, and dropped supplies to refugees in the wreck they had done so much to create.

Lancaster production stopped in February 1946, and the much smaller post-war Bomber Command re-equipped rapidly with Lincolns. By the end of 1946 the mass scrapping of Lancasters had started in earnest, although the type remained in Bomber Command service, with two squadrons in Malta and a specialised survey unit, until 1954. Coastal Command used the Lancaster for a rather longer period. The ASR.IIIs surplus to requirements after the dismantling of Tiger Force, along with other converted Mk III Lancasters, went to replace Coastal Command's Liberators, which had been returned to the USA under Lend-Lease at the end of the war. In 1949 they were updated to GR.III standard by the installation of air-to-surface-vessel (ASV) radar equipment. These remained in service with Coastal Command, finally as trainers, until October 1956. The last Lancaster on RAF strength was a single aircraft leased to Handley

Page until the early 1960s to test laminar-flow wing sections. It reverted to the RAF in the mid-1960s and is now the pride of the service's Historic Aircraft Flight.

The Royal Canadian Air Force continued to operate Lancasters for maritime-reconnaissance long after the war, the last Lancaster 10-MR being retired from a special squadron in 1964. Some were then sold as water-bombers for fighting forest fires, and one survivor was ferried back to a private collection in Britain in the late 1970s. Another large post-war Lancaster operator was the French Aéronavale, which used a batch of 54 B.Is and B.VIIs for maritime-reconnaissance from 1952 until they were replaced by P2V-7 Neptunes in the late 1950s. Fifteen Lancasters were delivered from RAF surplus stocks to the Argentine, and in mid-1966 one bomber was reported as still operational.

Most mysterious of all Lancaster operations, however, involved the unmarked aircraft sighted by an RAF Mosquito pilot off the French coast during the Berlin crisis of 1948–49. It was believed at the time that the Soviet Air Force might have retained a few Lancasters which, for one reason or another, had force-landed in Soviet-held territory, and was using them to probe radar defences.

Although the Lancaster's post-war career was to be small beer compared to its wartime achievements, it was to be followed by a long line of descendants. In 1945, as the last Lancasters started their journey down the assembly line, their career was only just beginning.

Derivatives and developments

The first-born of the Lancaster's long progeny was actually developed in parallel with the bomber – the Avro 685 York. The prototype York was produced in less than six months from the start of design work and first flew in July 1942, but at that time production was not approved because it would have reduced the industrial capacity available for Lancasters.

The York was a straightforward transport adaptation of the Lancaster, with the same wing, powerplant, tail unit and undercarriage married to a square-section transport fuselage slung beneath the wing. A central tailfin was added to the tail unit after flight trials, offsetting the effects of the larger front fuselage. A few Yorks were produced during the war years, but large-scale production did not begin until 1945. Production eventually totalled 256 aircraft, the last being delivered in April 1948. In the absence of any competitive British airliners, Yorks were used for passenger services in the Middle East and Africa by the British Overseas Airways Corporation. Later, BOAC relegated the type to freighting duties, finally disposing of its last Yorks in 1957. The aircraft nevertheless remained in use with independent airlines, often on trooping contracts, until the early 1960s. Most of the Yorks were built for RAF Transport Command, and many of these were sold to civil operators in various parts of the world.

An even more basic adaptation of the Lancaster was the Lancastrian. This was developed from the modified Lancaster IIIs used by Trans-Canada Airlines to operate a

Avro York (MW 295) at an RAF airbase in the Far East in the early '50s.

high-priority transatlantic passenger/freight service from July 1943. With all defensive armament and armour removed, the eight modified aircraft had a range of 4,150 miles (6,680 km). With the easing of pressure on Lancaster production in 1945, new airframes could be delivered to the same standard, for use as Lancastrians. BOAC operated 20 of the type on North Atlantic services and on a high-speed Kangaroo service to Sydney.

The Lancastrian's career was prolonged by the failure of its cousin the Tudor, and by British economic policy which restricted the import of better airliners from the United States. With only nine passenger seats (13 in later versions) in the cramped, unpressurised rear fuselage, the Lancastrian was scarcely a practical airliner, and in the absence of political pressure on BOAC and British South American Airways (BSAA) to buy British it is unlikely that it would ever have been produced in quantity. Some Lancastrians were delivered to Alitalia, Silver City Airways and Skyways, and some were used as tankers to carry fuel into Berlin during the Soviet blockade of 1948–49, but the last of them was retired in 1951.

The mainstream of Lancaster development had, however, taken a different course when production of the Lancastrian and York got under way. The decision to proceed with design and development of an improved, higher-flying Lancaster version using the then new two-stage-supercharged Rolls-Royce Merlin was taken in 1943, and prototypes of the Lancaster IV were ordered to Specification B.14/43.

To take advantage of the greater high-altitude output of the new engines, Roy Chadwick's team designed a new wing of greater span and area for the new Lancaster. To compensate for the greater weight and length of the new engines, and to restore stability and control with the larger

A civil transport Lancaster, operated by Trans-Canada Airlines, arrives at Prestwick after a transatlantic flight.

wing, the rear fuselage was slightly extended. The nose was redesigned to incorporate a more streamlined turret and an improved bomb-aiming position. The engines were installed in new-type "power eggs" with semi-annular radiators. The Lancaster IV was to have British-built Merlin 85 engines, and the Lancaster V was to be fitted with the equivalent Packard-built Merlin 66 or 68. In 1944 they were renamed Lincoln B.1 and B.2 respectively.

Development and production of the Lincoln took second place to increasing the output of Lancasters until late 1944, when it was planned to accelerate the production of the Lincoln so that the heavier, longer-range bomber would be available in time to form the backbone of the Tiger Force for bombing Japan. It was planned to wind down Lancaster production from November 1944, and to have more than 2,200 Lincolns completed by mid-1946.

The first Lincoln B.1 flew in June 1944, the second following in November. Development was not altogether smooth, the Merlin 85s giving trouble and the aircraft being plagued with vibration problems until four-blade propellers were fitted. Only about 50 aircraft had been flown by May 1945. With the end of the war, Lincoln production contracts were cut back sharply, the type being regarded as a stop-gap pending availability of the jet bombers ordered in 1945. Avro, Metropolitan-Vickers and Armstrong Whitworth participated in British production, but planned manufacture in Canada was terminated when the first Lincoln XV had been completed but not flown.

June 1945 saw the delivery of the first Lincoln B.2, and the Packard engines were found to be more reliable than the powerplants of the B.1. The later version was also better armed than the B.1, with twin 0.5 in (12.7 mm) machine-guns in the nose and tail and a dorsal Bristol B.17 turret, an electrically powered unit mounting a pair of 20 mm (0.79 in) Hispano cannon. It was decided in November that the B.1 would be used only for training and conversion, and most of the 82 production B.1s were scrapped without seeing service.

The first unit to take delivery of operational Lincolns in February 1946 was 44 Squadron, which had been the first recipient of the Lancaster just over four years earlier. Replacement of the Lancaster got under way in 1947, and a total of 447 Lincoln B.2s were built before production ended in 1948. Later some Lincolns were modified, with Mk 4A H2S equipment replacing the older Mk 3G, and the defensive armament was progressively reduced, most aircraft ending their careers with neither nose nor dorsal armament. The latter, with its twin cannon, was regarded as operationally effective, but its 1,500 lb (680 kg) weight and the complexity of its electrical drive and ammunition feed were drawbacks. Some Lincolns were fitted with bulged bomb doors to accommodate a Tallboy penetration bomb, and the type was tested with Grand Slam.

From the RAF's point of view, the Lincoln's most serious drawback was that its speed and altitude were not high enough to escape safely from the blast of a nuclear weapon, and in mid-1950 one Lincoln squadron converted to Boeing Washington B.1s acquired second-hand from the US Air Force. Other Lincoln squadrons started to convert to Canberras in the following year, and the type was ultimately replaced by the Vickers Valiant in 1955.

Between 1950 and 1955 the Lincoln was used for anti-terrorist operatons in Malaya and Kenya, and during and after the type's employment with Bomber Command the Lincoln was extensively used for second-line roles. Two were employed for the development of electronic equipment such as Green Cheese, a pioneering side-looking airborne radar. Others were used for probing Soviet radar defences, one aircraft being shot down over Germany by Soviet MiG-15s in March 1953 after it strayed across the Eastern zone. Two Lincolns were stripped down, fitted with high-altitude-rated

(Imperial War Museum)

Lancastrian I, serving with BOAC in the spring of 1945.

Lincoln B.I fitted with H2S radome under the rear fuselage.

Merlin 113s and used by the Royal Aircraft Establishment for drop tests of nuclear stores. A quite bewildering number of engines were tested in Lincolns. Suffice it to say that the Lincoln and Lancaster between them tested nearly every large jet or turboprop engine built in Britain in the 1940s and 1950s.

A few Lincolns were used for RAF policing duties in Aden in 1956–57, but after that the type was confined to second-line roles, the last aircraft remaining in service for electronic-countermeasures training until 1963. The Argentine was the only export customer for the Lincoln, acquiring 30 of the type – 12 were B.1s which had escaped the acetylene torch, while the remainder were new B.2s built by Armstrong Whitworth, and all were stripped of H2S and other equipment. Some were still in service as transports in the Argentine's sector of the Antarctic in the mid-1960s. Two more British-built Lincolns were converted to freighter configuration in 1957, being intended for a meat transport company in Peru, but they were never delivered or even flown before being scrapped in 1959.

Unlike Canada, Australia persisted with production plans for the Lincoln. It had been decided early in 1944 to abandon plans for Australian production of the Lancaster III in favour of the newer aircraft. The first Lincoln B.30 flew from the Government Aircraft Factories facility at Fisherman's Bend in March 1946. Later aircraft were fitted with Merlin 102s built by the Commonwealth Aircraft Company, and the last few were completed as MR.31 maritime-reconnaissance aircraft. These had the nose-gun turret removed, and to compensate for the change in centre of gravity the nose was extended by 78 in (198 cm) forward of the cockpit. Fitted with ASV Mk 7 radar, developed from H2S, the MR.31 stayed in production until 1953, the rate of production having been kept low in order to keep Australia's aircraft industry in being. The Mk 30 bombers saw some action in Malaya in 1956–58, and many were converted to MR.31 standard. The last Australian Lincolns were the MR.31s, which were replaced by Lockheed Neptunes in mid-1961.

Developed in parallel with the Lincoln, as the York had been developed alongside the Lancaster, the Avro Tudor was far less successful. Planned as a British answer to the contemporary American four-engined airliners, the Tudor combined the wing, engines and landing gear of the Lincoln with a circular-section pressurised fuselage and a new tail unit. Basically smaller and less powerful than the contemporary Constellation and DC-6 – which had been developed while the British industry unavoidably concentrated on military aircraft – the Tudor flew in June 1945. The transatlantic Tudor 1 was finally rejected by BOAC in April 1947 after a long series of modifications, and the corporation ordered bigger American aircraft instead. The aircraft on the production line were modified into Tudor 4s, for British South American Airways, but airworthiness approval was withdrawn after two of the type vanished over the Caribbean.

The other main Tudor version was designed for operations over shorter stage lengths of the BOAC Eastern route system. This, the Tudor 2, had a greatly lengthened and wider fuselage with seats for 60 passengers. By 1945 no fewer than 79 Tudor 2s were on order for BOAC, Qantas and South African Airways, but the aircraft proved overweight and underpowered after it flew in March 1946. Production orders had been cancelled by the time the prototype crashed in August 1947. Tragically, chief designer Roy Chadwick was among the dead. A few of the Tudor 4s were re-certificated and used for freight services in the 1950s, but the long-fuselage Tudor was never used in scheduled service.

The ultimate descendant of the Lancaster was designed to meet a Coastal Command requirement for a successor to the Lancaster GR.III. Originally designated Lincoln ASR.III, the new aircraft underwent extensive redesign to suit the maritime-reconnaissance role. The Merlins gave way to the more powerful Griffons, driving six-blade contra-rotating airscrews, while the existing wing was married to a slightly shorter, fatter fuselage to provide more room for radar equipment and better working conditions, and the tail was redesigned.

Manchester I

Power units
2 × Rolls-Royce Vulture II engines
 : 1,845 hp each at 5,000 ft (1,520 m)

Performance
Max speed at normal weight
 : 264 mph (425 km/h at 17,000 ft (5,180 m)
Cruising speed at overload weight
 : 205 mph (330 km/h) at 15,000 ft (4,570 m)
Service ceiling at mean weight
 : 19,300 ft (5,880 m)

Weights
Tare
 : 29,432 lb (13,350 kg)
Overload take-off
 : 50,000 lb (22,680 kg)

Dimensions
Span
 : 90 ft 1 in (27.46 m)
Length (tail up)
 : 68 ft 10 in (20.98 m)
Height
 : 19 ft 6 in (5.94 m)
Wing area
 : 1,131 sq ft (105.1 m²)

Armament
8 × 0.303 in (7.7 mm) machine-guns
2 × 1,900 lb (862 kg), 2 × 1,000 lb
(454 kg) and 3 × 250 lb (113 kg)
bombs

Crew
7

Lancaster B.Mk.I

Power units
4 × Rolls-Royce Merlin XX or 22 engines
 : 1,460 hp each at 6,250 ft (1,905 m)

Performance
Max speed at normal weight
 : 271 mph (436 km/h) at 6,250 ft (1,905 m)
Most economical cruising speed
 : 216 mph (348 km/h) at 20,000 ft (6,100 m)
Service ceiling at mean weight
 : 24,500 ft (7,470 m)

Weights
Tare
 : 36,900 lb (16,740 kg)
Max take-off
 : 72,000 lb (32,660 kg)

Dimensions
Span
 : 102 ft 0 in (31.09 m)
Length (tail up)
 : 69 ft 6 in (21.18 m)
Height (tail up)
 : 20 ft 6 in (6.25 m)
Wing area
 : 1,300 sq ft (120.8 m²)

Armament
8 (early aircraft: 10) × 0.303 in (7.7
mm) machine-guns
14 × 1,000 lb (454 kg) bombs

Crew
7

Lincoln B.2

Power units
4 × Packard-built Marlin 68A engines
: 1,750 hp each at 5,500 ft (1,680 m)

Performance
Max speed at full load
: 305 mph (491 km/h) at 19,000 ft (5,790 m)
Cruising speed at mean weight
: 244 mph (393 km/h at 22,500 ft (6,860 m)

Weights
Tare
: 44,188 lb (20.044 kg)
Max take-off
: 82,000 lb (37,200 kg)

Dimensions
Span
: 120 ft 0 in (36.58 m)
Length
: 78 ft 3 in (23.85 m)
Height (tail up)
: 20 ft 6 in (6.25 m)
Wing area
: 1,421 sq ft (132.0 m²)

Armament
2 × 20 mm cannon and 4 × 0.5 in
(12.7 mm) machine-guns
Bombs: Same as Lancaster

Crew
7

Shackleton MR.3

Power units
4 × Rolls-Royce Griffon 57A12 engines
: 2,450 hp each

Performance
Max speed at 85,000 lb (38,560 kg)
: 302 mph (486 km/h) at 12,000 ft (3,660 m)
Long range cruising speed
: 200 mph (322 km/h) at 1,500 ft (460 m)
Service ceiling
: 19,200 ft (5,850 m)

Weights
Tare
57,800 lb (26,220 kg)
Loaded
: 100,000 lb, approx. (45,360 kg)

Dimensions
Span
: 119 ft 10 in (36.53 m)
Length
: 92 ft 9 in (28.27 m)
Height
: 23 ft 4 in (7.11 m)
Wing area
:1,421 sq ft (132.0 m²)

Crew
11

Flown in March 1949, the new aircraft was renamed Shackleton MR.1. Seventy-seven MR.1s were followed, starting in 1952, by a batch of 69 MR.2s with improved operational equipment including a new radar with a retractable ventral scanner. The definitive development of the Shackleton was the MR.3 with a nosewheel undercarriage, further improved electronics and a modified wing. A proposed Shackleton MR.4 development with Napier Nomad compound diesel engines was not proceeded with, and production ended in 1960. From 1960 the Shackletons were brought up to MR.3 Phase 3 standards with auxiliary Viper jet engines in the outboard nacelles. These aircraft served until replaced by Nimrods in the early 1970s.

The line was not quite ended even with the Shackleton. The basic wing structure of the Lincoln was used in the Argosy freighter, with its twin tailbooms and four Dart turboprops. The commercial success expected for the Argosy failed to materialise, because its appearance in 1959 coincided with an influx of cheap DC-6s, DC-7s and Constellations on to the freight market as the big airlines bought jets. Fifty-six Argosy C.1s were acquired by the RAF, whose pilots christened the aircraft "the whistling wheelbarrow". Production ended in 1964, and the Argosys were retired from transport duties following a mid-1970s review of defence costs.

At the time of writing, a few Shackleton MR.3s remain in service with the South African Air Force, but they are not the sole survivors outside the museums of the line which started with specification P.13/36 nearly half a century ago. In the late 1960s, faced with the emerging threat of low-level Soviet strike aircraft with the range to reach Britain from East Germany or the northern USSR, the RAF decided to improvise an airborne early warning system to replace carrier-borne aircraft which Britain's abandonment of carriers had left without a base. The American-built APS-20F radars from the carrier-based Gannet aircraft were transplanted into stored Shackleton MR.2 airframes. The converted aircraft, the Shackleton AEW.2, entered service in 1972, and the somewhat primitive radar equipment has been slightly updated since then. The Shackletons are due to be replaced by the incomparably more advanced Nimrod AEW.3 in mid-1982. Until then, the last of the Lancaster line is as vital as ever to the defence of Britain.

Lancasters returning from a bombing mission.

(Imperial War Museum)